ICONS

★ICONS

igloo

igloo

Published in 2010
by Igloo Books Ltd
Cottage Farm
Sywell
NN6 0BJ

www.igloo-books.com

10 9 8 7 6 5 4 3 2 1
ISBN 978-0-85734-250-8

Authors: Judith Millidge and Jessica Hodge
Printed and manufactured in China

Contents

Introduction

What makes an icon? Icons were once religious objects of devotion, beautifully crafted, gilded representations of saints and holy people. Today, the word has come to mean someone, real or imaginary, who has come to symbolize a concept or an institution, whether it be political, religious or cultural.

All the people in this book stand out. They may have been the first, the best, or simply the most memorable person in their field, whether it is as a smoldering screen siren (Marilyn), an intrepid explorer (Sir Edmund Hillary), or the world's most famous and longest-lived cartoon character (Mickey Mouse). More than that, individually they have come to symbolize one particular aspect of their fame. Clark Gable, for example, is the archetypal Hollywood idol of the 1930s and 1940s; Michael Jordan epitomizes the winning, all-American sportsman; and Madonna is the embodiment of the high achieving rock chick. Icons not only excel in their work, they embody it and their success is so all consuming that the rest of us can only look on in awe.

Popular icons are a 20th-century innovation, made possible only by the mass media – film, television, record labels and newspapers. Earlier generations simply did not have such objects of veneration. Without the oxygen of publicity, stars cannot shine – or if they do, precious few people get to hear about them. Andy Warhol, the iconic pop artist, once said that everyone would be famous for 15 minutes, but for everyone in this book, that is a gross underestimation. Icons are not one-hit wonders, but people who prove, time and again, that they are excellent at what they do. Many a singer's career has hit the doldrums because public tastes change, but the really iconic – Cher, Tina Turner and Marvin Gaye, for example – often reinvent themselves, as times change. Others, such as David Bowie, are famous for their chameleon-like abilities to change their image; for some, like the great actor Laurence Olivier, it is this ability that helps define them.

Some icons – the Rolling Stones, Aretha Franklin, or Stevie Wonder – merit inclusion because of a longevity that enhances their stellar talents. However, other stars shine all too briefly, leaving a searing image burnt on the retinas of the world that can be replayed over and over, but never recaptured in their original glory. James Dean, Jimi Hendrix and Jim Morrison all bowed out at the height of their powers, leaving behind a memorable body of work, an eternally youthful image and a heavy cloud of nostalgia.

Selecting the list has not been easy and it is unlikely that any two people would come up with the same collection. The iconic stars in these pages share a number of qualities – undoubted talent, dedication, hard work and a bit of luck. All of them are famous for their achievements, unlike many recent celebrities who are famous simply for being famous.

True icons stand the test of time. They embody qualities that their fans want to emulate and their appeal is timeless, crossing continents and spanning generations.

Muhammad Ali

Born Cassius Marcellus Clay Jr.
January 17, 1942
Louisville, Kentucky, USA

Renowned American boxer and three times world heavyweight champion, Muhammad Ali has long been hailed as 'the Greatest'. His stunning record, unorthodox fighting style and gift of the gab have lifted him to superstar status.

Muhammad Ali (originally born, Cassisus Clay Jr.) was born in Louisville, Kentucky. His father, Cassius Marcellus Clay Sr., was named after a 19th-century Kentucky politician and anti-slavery campaigner. It was a local police officer and boxing coach who first encouraged the 12-year-old Cassius to box, when they found the boy fuming over the theft of his bicycle. As an amateur, Clay went on to win an astonishing 100 out of his 105 matches, culminating in a gold medal in the light heavyweight division at the 1960 Olympics in Rome.

After his Olympic triumph he turned professional. Perfecting his line in pre-match verbal hype, he won all 19 of his fights between 1960 and 1963, though there were some close calls. When he met world heavyweight champion, Sonny Liston, in Miami in February 1964, he was not widely tipped to win. At the weigh-in, Ali taunted Liston, famously saying that he would 'float like a butterfly, sting like a bee'. Unusually tall, at 190 cm (6 ft 3 in), he did not hold his hands high to protect his face in the accepted heavyweight style, but instead relied on speed, dexterity and his powerful jab. At 22, Ali's win against Liston made him the youngest boxer ever to take a title from a reigning heavyweight champion – in his own words, 'I shook up the world'. He shook it up some more in 1964, joining the, then controversial Nation, of Islam movement and adopting the name, Muhammad Ali. In early 1966, he responded to the Vietnam draft by declaring himself a conscientious objector. Found guilty of refusing to serve, he was stripped of his title and boxing license.

Ali appealed and the Supreme Court reversed his conviction in June 1971. He was allowed to fight again from 1970 and soon afterwards took part in three iconic bouts. He suffered his first professional loss against Joe Frazier in the hugely hyped 'Fight of the Century' on March 8, 1971. But the 'Rumble in the Jungle' in Zaire in October 1974, in one of the biggest upsets in boxing history, Ali regained his heavyweight title by outlasting and outclassing the champion, George Foreman. And in October 1975, in a final clash with Frazier billed as the 'Thrilla in Manila', he was the victor in the 15th and final round.

Ali retired in 1981, having defeated every top heavyweight of his time and was sadly diagnosed with Parkinson's disease in 1984. He has become a widely respected and loved public figure, working with the US civil rights movement and the United Nations. In 2005 he received the Presidential Medal of Freedom from President George W. Bush.

Left: Ali lands a winning punch on Floyd Patterson during their 1965 heavyweight title fight.

Below: Ali retained his fighting form until his retirement in 1981.

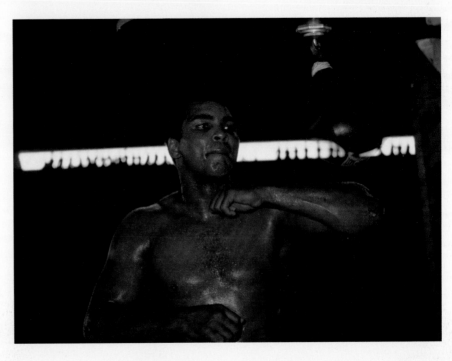

Woody Allen

Born Allen Stewart Konigsberg
December 1, 1935
Brooklyn, New York, USA

Actor, screenwriter, musician and playwright, the multi-talented Woody Allen is, above all, a prolific film director, who writes all his own films. He is one of the few American directors whose dominant creative role gives his many films, from romantic comedies to serious dramas, a highly distinctive style.

The only son of Orthodox Jewish parents, Allen grew up in a middle-class Brooklyn neighborhood. His devoted, quizzical relationship with New York remains one of the defining threads of his work, above all in *Manhattan* (1979), a black-and-white love song to his home city. His early film passions, never abandoned, were for the Marx Brothers and Humphrey Bogart. But his early career was as a comic – first as a contributor to radio shows and then on stage himself, as a stand-up comedian. His uniquely New York Jewish act defined the Allen persona – intellectual, insecure, neurotic and classically funny. Allen stepped into the movie world in 1965, when he was hired to write the screenplay for the sharp, farcical *What's New, Pussycat?*, in which he also had a role. Early stage work included his tribute to Bogart, *Play It Again, Sam*, which he filmed in 1972, launching his long association with his co-star, Diane Keaton.

His best-known work with Keaton, *Annie Hall* (1977), marked a move into more thoughtful and sophisticated territory, while retaining all Allen's entertaining satiric edge. It was a huge critical and box office success. Throughout his career, Allen has continued to play with different styles and techniques. Some of his less popular films of the 1970s and 1980s, such as *Interiors* (1978) and *September* (1987), showed the influence of European film directors, notably Ingmar Bergman.

His more mainstream work from this time, including the Oscar-winning *Hannah and Her Sisters* (1986) – inspired by his relationship with Mia Farrow – and *Crimes and Misdemeanors* (1989), also introduced a more serious, even tragic, tone alongside the comedy. This darker note recurs in the emotionally violent *Husbands and Wives* (1992), with its jumpy, hand-held camerawork and pessimistic view of enduring love. This was filmed during his very public break-up with Farrow.

Allen's response to personal upheaval was to revert to humor, with the comic thriller *Manhattan Murder Mystery* (1993) and the glorious period comedy *Bullets over Broadway* (1994). The latter depicted the lush theater world of the 1930s, an era which also featured in *Sweet and Lowdown* (1999). Allen continues to be prolific, but more recent work has had a mixed reception. *Match Point* (2005), the story of a social-climbing tennis pro, was an interesting development, being shot, not in Allen's beloved New York, but in London. And *Vicky Cristina Barcelona* (2008), again filmed in a new and evocative location, marked a full return to the intelligent, thoughtful, romantic comedies for which Allen is best loved.

Right: Woody Allen is one of America's most thought-provoking and interesting film directors.

Below: Allen with Diane Keaton on the set of *Annie Hall*, (1977).

Pedro Almodóvar

Born Pedro Almodóvar
Caballero
September 25, 1949
Calzada de Calatrava,
Cuidad Real, Spain

A self-taught Spanish film-maker, the openly gay Pedro Almodóvar has come a long way from his backwoods origins in provincial Spain. Acclaimed for his flamboyant plotting, melodramatic storylines and subtle and perceptive roles for women, he is regarded by many as the most inspired and prolific Spanish film-maker of his day.

Determined from childhood to make movies, Almodóvar began his career in 1960s Madrid, where the dictator, General Franco, had just closed the National School of Cinema. His first short films, made with a hand-held camera, were outrageously melodramatic and overtly sexual, in part, no doubt, a protest against an oppressive regime. His early work also shows the influence of Hollywood film noir and screwball comedy.

With Franco's death in 1975, Almodóvar became a leading light in Madrid's cultural renaissance, working with Carmen Maura, the first of several actresses with whom he established a creative partnership and the then unknown Antonio Banderas.

The sex-and-death-fixated *Matador* (1986) and the stylish and complex *Law of Desire* (1987) used extreme and shocking content to make serious points. The light comedy *Women on the Verge of a Nervous Breakdown* (1988) was Almodóvar's international breakthrough, while *High Heels* (1991) was an early example of his fascination with fractured female relationships, here between a self-involved mother and the daughter she abandoned.

A key transitional film is *The Flower of My Secret* (1995), which focuses on a neglected wife finding her own path to self-esteem. It paved the way for the trio of increasingly confident films that made Almodóvar's international reputation. *Live Flesh* (1997) saw his first collaboration with Penélope Cruz, who has since became another of his regulars, while *All About My Mother* (1999), revisiting the now familiar themes of sisterhood and family, won more awards and honors than any other Spanish film and established Almodóvar in the movie mainstream. The daring *Talk to Her* (2002), a potentially bleak tale of two men caring for women in comas, unfolds in a delicate series of flashbacks and is a moving reflection on the nature of love and devotion. It won Almodóvar an Oscar for its screenplay.

Family relationships also form the theme of the 2006 *Volver*, a tragi-comic tale of female solidarity and resilience, shot in the rural Spain of the director's childhood. It unites two of Almodóvar's best-loved muses: Carmen Maura plays a feckless mother and Penélope Cruz gives a career-best, Oscar-nominated performance as her grown-up daughter.

Broken Embraces (2009), again starring Cruz, is Almodóvar's longest and most expensive movie to date. It features a complex and opaque structure of flashback and film-within-film, which has become one of Almodóvar's signature notes.

Left: Almodóvar directing the psychological drama, *La Flor de Mi Secreto* (*The Flower of My Secret*), 1995.

Below: Almodóvar is the best known Spanish film-maker of his generation and his movies have a huge international following.

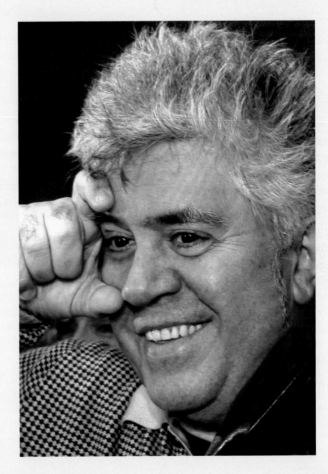

Fred Astaire

Born Frederick Austerlitz
May 10, 1899
Omaha, Nebraska, USA

Died June 22, 1987
Los Angeles, California,
USA

Debonair, charming and extraordinarily graceful, Fred Astaire was the ultimate Hollywood song-and-dance man. He revolutionized dance on camera, both as a solo dancer and paired with a succession of dancing actresses, most famously Ginger Rogers.

In his signature top hat, white tie and tails, Astaire was a popular romantic lead in the 1930s and 1940s, despite his lack of movie-star good looks. He also made some of the best-loved films of the time, from *Top Hat* with Rogers (1935) to *Silk Stockings* with Cyd Charisse (1957).

Astaire's career began at the tender age of seven, as a vaudeville partner to his older sister, Adele. The pair made it to Broadway in 1917, working with the Gershwins and starring in shows such as *Lady Be Good* (1924) and *Funny Face* (1927). Following Adele's marriage and retirement in 1932, Hollywood came calling in the form of David O. Selznick, who signed Astaire to RKO and partnered him with Ginger Rogers, in a sequence of unmatchable films which elevated both leads to stardom. Katharine Hepburn reportedly said: 'He gives her class, she gives him sex.' Astaire's light tenor married well with Rogers' breathy soprano, but it was the quality of the dancing that set their films apart. The choreography, by Astaire and Hermes Pan, introduced dance as an intrinsic element of the Hollywood film musical; six of the nine musicals Astaire created for RKO became their biggest moneymakers.

Astaire's work with later song-and-dance partners tends to get overshadowed by the glamor and nostalgia of the Astaire/Rogers years. But his movie work continued to be fresh and innovative. *Broadway Melody of 1940* featured an extended dance routine with the brilliant tap-dancer Eleanor Powell, who was Astaire's first partner after Rogers. *You'll Never Get Rich* (1941), with Rita Hayworth, allowed Astaire to introduce Latin American dance rhythms into his routines and after a brief retirement in 1946, he came storming back to make *Easter Parade* (1949) opposite Judy Garland. His co-stars in the 1950s included Jane Powell, Leslie Caron and Audrey Hepburn (*Funny Face*, 1957).

After 30 musical films in 25 years, Astaire turned in the 1960s and 1970s to a series of Emmy-winning music and dance specials made for television and to straight film. He received his only Oscar nomination, as Best Supporting Actor, for his role in *The Towering Inferno* (1974).

As a singer, Astaire introduced and left his mark on classics such as *Fascinating Rhythm*, *Foggy Day*, and *Nice Work if You Can Get It*. As a virtuoso dancer, with superb technical control and an innate sense of rhythm, he drew his influences from a wide range of sources, from tap dance to ballet to ballroom. The result was his uniquely personal 'outlaw style,' which is still influential today.

Left: Astaire and Ginger Rogers at their most glamorous, 1949. They starred together in ten films.

Right: 'I'm just a hoofer with a spare set of tails,' said Fred Astaire, whose long career lasted an incredible 76 years.

Sir David Attenborough

A naturalist, broadcaster and television pioneer, Sir David Attenborough is among the most outstanding and best-loved broadcasters of his generation. Knighted by Queen Elizabeth II in 1985, he has many other civic and academic honors to his name.

After a science degree at Cambridge and national service in the Royal Navy, Attenborough joined the BBC as a trainee in 1952, the very early days of television. His long association with natural history programs began in 1954, as the presenter of *Zoo Quest*. After leaving the BBC in the early 1960s, he was summoned back in a surprise move in 1965 as Controller of BBC2. This new channel had been launched the previous year but was struggling to find its feet.

Attenborough's clear sense of what publicly funded broadcasting should offer galvanized BBC2; he established a diverse range of programs that defined the channel for decades. Commissions included classics, such as the quiz show *Call My Bluff*, the self-help *Money Programme* and the revolutionary late-night contemporary music program, *The Old Grey Whistle Test*. To mark the advent of color, he commissioned a landmark and hugely successful 13-part history of western art, *Civilisation*, introduced by art historian, Kenneth Clark. This was followed by two further authored documentaries, Jacob Bronowski's *The Ascent of Man* and Alistair Cooke's *America*.

But at heart, Attenborough was a program-maker and his promotion in 1969 to Director of Programmes left him little time for filming. In 1973, he resigned to return to documentary making and writing. He had begun planning the *Life on Earth* series while still a manager and was now able to take on the role of presenter himself. His committed and serious approach to film-making engaged the interest and co-operation of the scientific community, gaining his team privileged access – who can forget Attenborough with Dian Fossey's research group of mountain gorillas? Novel film-making techniques were developed, too, to get the shots he wanted and the result is television history, with the series still retailing on DVD today.

The success of *Life on Earth* encouraged the BBC to commission a new series, *The Living Planet*, screened in 1984 and focusing on how living organisms adapt to their environment. *The Trials of Life* (1990) looked at animal behavior, causing some audience consternation with its depiction of the realities of hunter and hunted. Still on a roll, Attenborough then turned his attention to more specialized areas of the natural world, beginning with

> **Born** David Frederick Attenborough
> May 8, 1926
> London, England

The Private Life of Plants (1995), which again required ingenious camerawork, as well as time-lapse techniques, to bring its subject alive. *The Life of Birds* (1998), *The Life of Mammals* (2002), *Life in the Undergrowth* (2005) and *Life in Cold Blood* (2008) all followed. The result is a consistent and encyclopaedic body of natural history programs that have become a benchmark of quality, technical innovation and intellectual rigor.

Left: The elder statesman of natural history broadcasting, Attenborough set the standard by which all others are judged.

Below: Attenborough with a llama at London Zoo in 1980, the year after his landmark series, *Life on Earth*.

The Beatles

Founded January 1960
Disbanded 1970

Members:
George Harrison 1943–2001
John Lennon 1940–1980
Paul McCartney 1942–Present
Ringo Starr (born Richard Starkey)
1940–Present

Perhaps the most famous, commercially successful and critically acclaimed British rock band ever, The Beatles redirected the history of western popular culture and music. Their style was rooted in skiffle and rock, but developed into an innovative, sophisticated and genre-busting musical idiom as the group's songwriting skills, range and musical intelligence grew. Singles hits included *She Loves You*, *Can't Buy Me Love*, and *A Hard Day's Night*, but The Beatles' legacy was assured by a sequence of revolutionary albums.

In their early days as a gifted, wisecracking rock-and-roll group, The Beatles revolutionized the sound and style of British popular music with their original and catchy synthesis of rock music, rhythm and blues. They first appeared in the clubs of Liverpool – their home city – and Hamburg. On the way, they lost two early band members - bassist, Stuart Sutcliffe and drummer, Pete Best. They acquired drummer, Ringo Starr, in 1962 to make up the Fab Four of fame and fable.

Molded by manager Brian Epstein from 1962, they adopted their signature mop-head haircuts and collarless suit-jackets and were signed to the EMI Parlophone label by prescient music producer, George Martin. Their debut album *Please Please Me*, recorded in a single session at the iconic Abbey Road Studios, became their first No. 1 hit. In total, 11 studio albums and 17 singles went on to reach the top spot in the British charts – an astonishing record.

Beatlemania went global, when the band toured the USA in spring 1964 and they entered the movie world with their mock-documentary *A Hard Day's Night* (1964) and its successors *Help!* (1965) and *A Magical Mystery Tour* (1967). A succession of landmark albums followed. *Rubber Soul* (1965) featured elements drawn from the contemporary US folk scene and from world music, notably in its use of the sitar, while *Revolver* (1966) further extended their range, from classical to psychedelic rock. The phenomenal concept album *Sgt. Pepper's Lonely Hearts Club Band* (1967) is regularly listed as one of the greatest albums of all time.

A creative period of transcendental meditation at a retreat in India led to *The White Album* (1968, formally called *The Beatles*). However, it also increased personal tensions within the group, which became focused on John Lennon's relationship with the artist, Yoko Ono.

Two further acclaimed albums followed, *Abbey Road* (1969) and *Let It Be* (1970), but in April 1970, Paul McCartney announced he was quitting the band and he filed for formal dissolution at the end of the year. All four members went on to make solo albums and McCartney developed a hugely successful post-Beatles career.

In the years that followed the band's dissolution, two tragic events happened. Lennon was killed in 1980 in New York City and George Harrison died of cancer in 2001.

Right: The fab four in 1964.

Below: The Beatles wave to thousands of fans at London Airport, 1965. As Paul said, 'We didn't all get into music for a job! We got into music to avoid a job, in truth – and get lots of girls.'

Boris Becker

A tennis phenomenon, Boris Becker astonished the sports world in 1985, by becoming the first unseeded player and the first German, to win the coveted men's singles title at Wimbledon, aged just 17.

Becker had won his first top-level singles title at the Queen's Club, London, only a fortnight earlier, having turned professional the previous year. When he won at Wimbledon, he was the youngest ever male Grand Slam singles champion. But this was no brief flowering – he went on to cement his reputation by taking the singles title at the Cincinnati Open two months later, in August 1985, again the youngest winner ever. The following year, he successfully defended his Wimbledon title in straight sets against Ivan Lendl and went on to win four more Grand Slams in a sparkling career.

His game was a dramatic, serve-and-volley affair, featuring a powerful and accurate serve, delivered with an unusual rocking movement; its pace earned him the nicknames 'Boom Boom' and 'Der Bomber'. Well built and strong, Becker was also a speedy mover about the court, diving for apparently unreachable volleys and sometimes calling on his powerful forehand to out-hit opponents from the baseline. The fast surfaces of grass and carpet courts suited him best.

After two successive Wimbledon wins, 1987 saw him knocked out in the second round of the tournament, though he was ranked number 2 in the world, while in 1988, he lost in the final to Stefan Edberg. Perhaps his best year was 1989, when he clinched two Grand Slam singles wins over his two main rivals, Edberg at Wimbledon and Lendl at the US Open. This, with his sterling performance for Germany in the Davis Cup, led the ATP World Tour to crown him Player of the Year.

However, the world number 1 slot eluded Becker for almost the whole of his career, apart from a brief period in 1991, after he defeated Lendl to win the Australian Open for the first time. Pete Sampras deprived him of a Wimbledon win in 1995, but he took his sixth Grand Slam title the following year, beating Michael Chang in the final of the Australian Open.

Becker was an emotional as well as a dramatic player, whose readily recognizable strokes have led to a whole new terminology among fans and commentators – from the 'Becker Blocker,' his early return shot, through the 'Becker Hecht,' his flying lunge, to the 'Becker Shuffle,' his dance of triumph after an important point.

Since his retirement from professional tennis, Becker has had a successful career as a businessman and tennis commentator.

Born Boris Franz Becker
November 22, 1967
Leimen, Federal Republic
of Germany

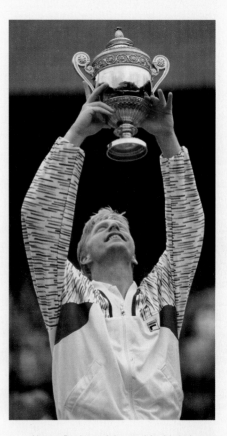

Above: Becker celebrates his third victory in the Mens' Singles at Wimbledon, 1989. His previous wins were in 1985 and 1986.

Left: Becker demonstrates his extraordinary reach, here defeating Ivan Lendl in 1985.

David Beckham

Born May 2, 1975
London, England

One of the great soccer legends of the early 21st century, David Beckham has enjoyed a global career. He has played with some of the best clubs in the world, as well as achieving every English footballer's dream of captaining the national squad. At one time the world's highest paid footballer, he was also the first to play in 100 Champions League matches.

Beckham was born in Leytonstone in east London and signed for Manchester United, the club he idolized, as a trainee in 1991. He was a dedicated player, constantly working to improve on his exceptional natural ability and was quickly rewarded with a place in the first team squad in 1992, making his Premier League debut in 1995. Sir Alex Ferguson, the manager of Manchester United, has always believed in exploring the talent of the club's young players and Beckham was fortunate to be one of a group of players nicknamed 'Fergie's Fledglings.'

He repaid his manager's faith many times over, probably most dramatically at the start of the 1996 season when, playing as a midfielder, he scored a goal from the halfway line against Wimbledon, a remarkable feat, unmatched even by the legendary Pelé Beckham was a vital member of Manchester United's team during the record-breaking 1998–9 season, when they achieved the triple crown of winning the Premiership, the FA Cup and the European Cup. Beckham's best season with United was in 2001–2, when he scored 11 goals in 28 league appearances.

In 2003, he moved to Real Madrid in a £25 million deal and in 2007, announced his move to California to play for the Los Angeles Galaxy team, a move that many believed would signal the end of his soccer career. However, Beckham bounced back and in 2009, was on loan to Italian side Milan.

Beckham made his first appearance for England in 1996 and from 1998 was a regular member of the squad. He was captain of the national side from 2000 to 2006 and by 2009, was the country's most capped player, with 115 appearances for the national team. Vilified and adored in almost equal measure during his 14-year England career, Beckham has rescued England more than once with his trademark curving goals and penalties.

Personable and handsome, Beckham pursues his soccer career side-by-side with his life as a dedicated ambassador for British sport in general and as an international celebrity (thanks in no small part to his wife, former Spice Girl, Victoria). He has also been generous with his support for young players with the establishment of the David Beckham Football Academies in London and Los Angeles. But it is his soccer exploits, his determination, passion and professionalism, that have made him one of the best players in the history of the beautiful game.

Right: Beckham playing for Real Madrid in June 2007.

Below: Away from the football pitch, David and Victoria Beckham are international celebrities and are highly sought-after by fashion designers, health and fitness specialists and others who want them to endorse their products.

The Bee Gees

Established 1958

Members:
Barry Gibb 1946– Present
Robin Gibb 1949– Present
Maurice Gibb 1949–2003

In a long and checkered career, The Bee Gees have survived changing fashions, derision and adulation to earn a place as one of the most influential bands of the late 20th century.

Born in Douglas on the Isle of Man, the Gibb brothers were brought up in Queensland, Australia, where they began to perform as a singing trio. The Bee Gees have enjoyed two main phases of popularity. The first, in the late 1960s, produced (among others) the singles *New York Mining Disaster* and *To Love Somebody* - a plaintive ballad that has since been covered by hundreds of artists, including Nina Simone, Janis Joplin and Michael Bolton. In 1969, Robin Gibb left to go solo, but the brothers reunited in 1971 and early in 1975, recorded *Jive Talkin*, the first record to feature what became their signature falsetto sound. The release of the soundtrack to the 1977 movie *Saturday Night Fever* made the Bee Gees global stars. Their vocals featured the trademark high-pitched Bee Gee harmonies, together with a fast moving disco beat and the brothers Gibb were photographed in clinging white shirts, with a flash of medallion nestling below their beards and their dazzling white teeth, framed by flowing locks. *Stayin' Alive, How Deep is Your Love, Tragedy* and *You Should be Dancing* defined the disco era and the album *Saturday Night Fever* sold over 40 million copies, becoming the biggest selling soundtrack album of the time.

As the disco era faded into a much-mocked memory, The Bee Gees' popularity declined, but their songwriting skills remained as strong as ever. Nothing they released in the 1980s was as successful as their 1970s output and the brothers suffered from an image problem as much as anything – popular taste had simply changed. Only *You Win Again* (1987) came near to recapturing their earlier commercial success.

During the 1990s, they produced several successful records and launched a series of 'One Night Only' concerts around the world, despite Maurice's battle with alcoholism and Barry's arthritis, which threatened to end his guitar playing. Nostalgia for their distinctive sound meant that by the turn of the century they had recaptured both critical and commercial success.

Sadly, Maurice died suddenly in 2003 in Miami, Florida. The two surviving brothers celebrate some 50 years in show business, with over 120 million albums sold worldwide, their detractors are forced to acknowledge The Bee Gees' astonishing success as prolific songwriters and one of the most popular bands of all time. Their longevity is a tribute to their unerring skills as songwriters – over 2,000 artists have recorded their songs, an extraordinary tribute to their versatility and talent.

Left: The Bee Gees have sold over 205 million records and singles during the course of their 50-year career.

Below: Although Barry Gibb claimed, 'I never really did any disco dancing,' The Bee Gees are forever associated with the disco era of the 1970s.

Humphrey Bogart

Born Humphrey DeForest
Bogart
December 25, 1899
New York City, USA

Died January 14, 1957
Los Angeles, California,
USA

Neither classically handsome, nor especially versatile, Humphrey Bogart was in many ways an unlikely star. Yet 'Bogie' became one of the Hollywood greats, cornering the market in playing tough, world-weary, yet compellingly decent characters. He appeared in 75 films, among them some of the great classics of the 1940s and 1950s, such as *The African Queen*, *The Treasure of the Sierra Madre* and most notably, *Casablanca*.

After military service in the US Navy in World War I, Bogart returned home to New York, where he got a job as a theatrical manager. He made his Broadway acting debut in 1922 and was reasonably successful, playing juvenile leads, or supporting roles. After the Wall Street Crash of 1929, the lights on Broadway dimmed, as the number of stage productions declined. It seemed to the acting community on the East Coast, that fame and fortune were easier to attain in Hollywood. Like many of his contemporaries, Bogart moved to California in search of work.

In 1930 he appeared in his first film, *Up the River*, alongside Spencer Tracy, playing the first of many tough-guy roles. He spent the next five years traveling between Hollywood and Broadway, but finally achieved a breakthrough with *The Petrified Forest* (1936), in which he played Duke Mantee, another ex-con. Critics praised his performance and Warner Brothers signed him as a contract player for $550 a week.

Bogart appeared in a succession of B movies, usually typecast as a cynical, underworld figure. It took him time to graduate to leading roles, but finally, in 1941, John Huston cast him as Roy 'Mad

Dog' Earle in *High Sierra*. Following the success of *The Maltese Falcon*, in which Bogart appeared as the fast-talking detective Sam Spade, he was cast as Rick Blaine, the tortured, world-weary nightclub owner in *Casablanca*. The movie won the Oscar for Best Picture in 1943 and Bogart's performance opposite Ingrid Bergman – his first romantic lead – is one of the most memorable of his career.

Bogart went on to play brave anti-heroes, notably in *To Have and Have Not* (1944), in which he appeared with the young Lauren Bacall. She captivated him and for the first time, Bogart had an affair with his leading lady. They married in 1945.

In the movies of his last years – *The Treasure of the Sierra Madre* (1948), *The Caine Mutiny* (1954) and *The African Queen* (for which he won an Oscar in 1951) – Bogart gave some of his best performances. His early death from cancer, at the age of 57, ended one of the most interesting careers in Hollywood. Bogart's restrained, yet compelling, screen presence set him apart from other actors and his intelligent and reliable performances gave him a lasting and powerful appeal to generations of movie lovers.

David Bowie

One of the most innovative rock stars of the 1970s and 1980s, David Bowie succeeded in presenting not one, but several iconic faces to the public.

From the androgynous Ziggy Stardust to the glittering Aladdin Sane and on to the ascetic Thin White Duke, Bowie reinvented his image several times during his career. Yet in these different guises, time and again, Bowie proved that he was more than capable of producing arresting songs that wowed his fans and exercised an enormous influence over his peers. Unafraid to experiment with different musical styles, Bowie has enjoyed amazing commercial success, as well as critical acclaim. Throughout his 40-year career he has sold over 136 million albums and remains in the top ten best-selling acts in British pop history. He has recorded with some of the best singers in the business, from Bing Crosby to Mick Jagger and Queen, as well as appearing in over 30 movies.

Born David Jones in south London, Bowie changed his surname early in his career to avoid being mistaken for Davy Jones of The Monkees. The single *Space Oddity*, released to coincide with the moon landing of 1969, was a top five hit in the UK and kick-started Bowie's years of fame. His albums *The Man Who Sold the World* (1970) and *Hunky Dory* (1971) demonstrated a wide variety of musical influences and styles, from the charming, if fey, *Kooks*, through the raw *Song for Bob Dylan* to *Queen Bitch*, one of the earliest glam rock numbers. The concept album *The Rise and Fall of Ziggy Stardust and the Spiders from Mars* (1972) pushed the glam rock theme still further, with Bowie resplendent in sparkling jump suits, flamboyant make-up and a red mullet hairstyle. A year later, he

achieved his first No. 1 album in the UK with *Aladdin Sane* and for the publicity, maintained his persona as Ziggy Stardust. But he soon left Ziggy behind and his work became more soul-based on *Young Americans*. Next came a diversion into the electro-synthesizer world of the Thin White Duke – an extension of the character Bowie played in the 1976 cult science fiction movie *The Man Who Fell to Earth* – on Station to Station and the three albums known as the 'Berlin Trilogy' (1977–9).

During the early 1980s, he moved on yet again, writing commercially popular rock numbers for *Let's Dance* in 1983. He formed a new band, Tin Machine, in 1989, which received a lukewarm reception, in contrast to his immensely popular 'Sound and Vision' stadium tour of 1991. True to form, he experimented with grunge, rap, dance and Indie music

Born	David Robert Haywood Jones
	January 8, 1947
	London, England

in the 1990s and early 2000s with varying degrees of success.

Bowie stands out among pop stars as a writer of intellectual rigor, great imagination and terrific innovation. Few have reinvented themselves so often and so successfully, while pursuing a long career at the top of their field.

Left: Ziggy Stardust, David Bowie's alter-ego during the 1970s.

Below: David Bowie assumed a more sophisticated and suave persona during the *Let's Dance* years of the early 1980s.

Don Bradman

Born Donald George Bradman
August 27, 1908
Cootamundra, New South
Wales, Australia

Died February 25, 2001
Kensington Park,
Adelaide, Australia

Few sporting icons are regarded with such reverential affection as Don Bradman. He is certainly the greatest Australian cricketer in the history of the game and according to many, the best cricketer ever.

Bradman was a remarkable batsman and even 70 years after his glory days in the 1930s, when he and the Australian cricket team trounced the English in a succession of Test matches, his achievements are unequalled. He remains a sporting hero in Australia and was hailed as 'the greatest living Australian' by the prime minister in 2001.

Don Bradman was born in New South Wales in 1908 and according to legend, honed his cricket skills by practicing with a golf ball and a cricket stump for a bat. He had natural talent, huge enthusiasm and exceptional powers of concentration and ambition that propelled him very quickly from the amateur game to the Australian national team. Having played for New South Wales from the age of 18, he made his Test debut just two years later in 1928.

The Australian tour of England in 1930–31 is the stuff of legend, entirely because of Bradman's performance, which was nothing short of astonishing. At Lords, in the first Test match, Bradman became the youngest player to score a Test century and in the first day of play at the third Test at Headingley, Leeds, he notched up a remarkable 309 runs. Many years later, when looking back over his career, Bradman recalled, 'In a long career there are many outstanding memories, but I suppose the opening day of the third Test at Leeds must rank as the greatest in my cricketing life. To do so against Australia's oldest and strongest rival was satisfying.'

Bradman appeared almost invincible at the wicket and opponents struggled to get him out. For the 1932–3 Test series in Australia, the English devised a controversial new strategy, bowling short balls aimed at the body, which became known as 'Bodyline'. It was devastatingly effective: Bradman averaged just 56 runs per innings instead of his usual 95 batting average, but it was dangerous and was quickly banned as unsporting.

Bradman became an Australian celebrity and was mobbed wherever he went. Known affectionately as 'The Don', he was a naturally shy man who hated the publicity. Nor was he universally popular among his teammates, some of whom envied his talents.

He retired from first class cricket in 1949 after captaining Australia's 'Invincibles', the team that toured England entirely unbeaten in the 1948–9 season and was knighted the same year. Sir Donald remained an influential figure in Australian cricket for the rest of his long life, as a commentator, selector and administrator and 60 years after the end of his career, many of his sporting records still remain unbroken.

Right: Bradman (on the right) strolls out to bat alongside Bill Woodfull, during the Australian tour of Britian in 1934

Below: Don Bradman proudly holds up a silver cup for the World Record Cricket score, awarded in March 1930 for scoring 452 runs while playing for New South Wales aganst Queensland

Marlon Brando

Born Marlon Brando Jr.
April 3, 1924
Omaha, Nebraska, USA

Died July 1, 2004
Los Angeles, California, USA

Marlon Brando's brooding good looks and carefully considered 'Method' acting first brought him acclaim in the 1950s and he is still seen as one of the finest Hollywood actors of all time. His performances in *A Streetcar Named Desire* (1951) and *On the Waterfront* (1954) catapulted him to the Hollywood A list and the picture of him astride his Triumph motorbike in *The Wild One* (1953) is one of the most iconic images in cinema history.

Brando was born in Omaha, Nebraska and after dropping out of high school and military academy, moved to New York. There he studied acting at the New School, under the influential Lee Strasberg and Stella Adler. He made his Broadway debut in 1944 and was voted Broadway's Most Promising Actor in 1946 for his role in *Truckline Café*. His breakthrough came with his magnetic and influential performance as Stanley Kowalski in the original 1947 production of Tennessee Williams' play *A Streetcar Named Desire*, which propelled him from Broadway to Hollywood. He played the same role on film in 1951, which won him an Oscar nomination for Best Actor.

His third Hollywood movie, *The Wild One* (1953), projected the unforgettable image of a leather-clad biker Brando on to the public consciousness. The malign influence of the angry, rebellious young man was viewed with trepidation and the film was actually banned for 14 years in Britain.

Brando won his first Oscar for *On the Waterfront* (1954) and then tried to work against type in a series of movies that demonstrated his range and versatility: he took to song-and-dance routines in *Guys and Dolls* (1955), tackled a serious

historical subject as Napoleon in *Désirée* and played an effete Fletcher Christian in *Mutiny on the Bounty* (1962). *Mutiny* reinforced Brando's reputation as a difficult actor and the film shoot went massively over budget and deadline, partly because Brando took over as director.

None of Brando's work in the 1960s was received with much enthusiasm by either critics, or audiences, but his portrayal of the Mafia boss Don Vito Corleone, in the classic 1972 movie *The Godfather* demonstrated a return to his earlier form. It also earned him his second Oscar – which he declined for political reasons. He received a seventh Oscar nomination for his performance in Bernardo Bertolucci's *Last Tango in Paris* (1973), which has been described as the best of his career. It turned out to be his last critically acclaimed movie, though there

were cameo roles in *Apocalypse Now* (1979) and *Superman* (1978).

Brando's eccentricities and chronic weight problems meant that he worked only intermittently for the rest of his life. However, acknowledged by his peers as a great actor, his influence still permeates Hollywood. 'The only thing an actor owes his public is not to bore them' he once remarked and he could never be accused of that.

Left: *The Wild One*, 1953.

Below: As Stanley Kowalski in *A Streetcar Named Desire*.

James Brown

Born James Joseph Brown Jr.
May 3, 1933
Barnwell, South Carolina,
USA

Died December 25, 2006
Atlanta, Georgia, USA

Famous for his flamboyant, energetic and passionate performances, James Brown was one of the most successful black artists of the 1960s and 1970s.

His funky soul hits brought dance music alive and made him one of the most original and influential artists in 20th-century music. Only Elvis Presley enjoyed more US chart entries than Brown. He was a prolific writer and much-imitated performer, with some 800 songs in his repertoire. As 'the Godfather of Soul', he also worked tirelessly throughout his career, earning himself another title, 'the hardest working man in show business.'

Born in South Carolina, during the segregation era, James Brown had a difficult and impoverished upbringing. He ended up in jail at the age of 16, after being convicted of an armed robbery.

While in prison, he learned to sing and perform with the prison gospel group and on his release, he joined a group called the Gospel Starlighters. They moved into secular music, renamed themselves the, Famous Flames and scored an R&B Top Ten hit in 1956, with *Please, Please, Please*, penned by Brown. For the next few years, Brown recorded gospel-inspired R&B music, combining frenzied lead vocals with complicated backing riffs. His first mainstream hit came in 1962 with the release of *Night Train* and in 1963 he achieved national recognition with his live album, *Live at the Apollo*, which sold an astonishing one million copies.

Brown became famous for his dramatic and well-choreographed stage acts. He also broke out of the restrictive mold of black R&B by establishing his own production company, Fair Deal, to promote his work more widely. The complex rhythms of his songs and the repetition of vocal phrases proved hugely influential in the world of funk music, but he also achieved mainstream success with two songs in 1965 and 1966 that came to define his act – *Papa's Got a Brand New Bag* and *I Got You (I Feel Good)*.

In the era of the Black Power movement in the USA, Brown added his voice to that of other black celebrities. He recorded *Say it Loud – I'm Black and Proud* in 1968, as well as lending a calming presence to the race riots that erupted in the wake of Martin Luther King's assassination.

By the early 1980s a younger generation of rap and hip hop artists, heavily influenced by Brown, was displacing him. Brown switched his talents to the movies and continued to tour relentlessly. His colorful private life merely added to his legendary status as one of the most exciting performers in the world. His concert performances were renowned – long, loud, visual extravaganzas with vigorous dance routines and unforgettable vocals. He continued performing right up to his sudden death on Christmas Day 2006.

Right: The Godfather of Soul in 1981.

Left: Brown performing at the Rock and Roll Hall of Fame show, 1995.

Mariah Carey

Born March 27, 1970
Huntingdon, New York,
USA

Mariah Carey is one of the most successful female recording artists of all time, her unique blend of R&B, pop and soul music, winning millions of fans around the world.

From her debut in 1990, Mariah Carey's powerful five-octave voice and songwriting abilities shot her straight to the top of the music charts. Her first five singles, starting with *Vision of Love*, all reached No. 1 in the Billboard chart – making her the only artist to have achieved this. She has had 18 No. 1 hits in the USA, placing her ahead of Elvis Presley and only just behind The Beatles in the musical league tables.

Carey was born in Huntingdon, Long Island. Her mother was an Irish-American opera singer, her father a black Venezuelan engineer. Her musical talents were clear from childhood, when she copied her mother singing snatches of opera around the house. Moving to New York City at 17, Mariah worked as a waitress, while cutting a demo tape and working as a backing singer. Columbia Records executive, Tommy Mottola, signed her in 1988, immediately after hearing her demo tape and she released her first album, *Mariah Carey*, in 1990. With four No. 1 singles from this album alone, Carey won Grammy awards in 1991 for Best New Artist and Best Female Vocalist. Mottola continued to manage her career and they married in 1993.

Carey became the most successful female singer of the 1990s, selling more than eight million

copies of each of her first three albums (*Mariah Carey*, *Emotions* and *Music Box*) and achieving a series of No. 1 hits. Specializing in emotive ballads and dance pop songs, she is often compared to Whitney Houston, but claims that her greatest influences are Billie Holiday, Gladys Knight and Aretha Franklin. From the mid-1990s she began incorporating elements of hip-hop into her work, telling critics who accused her of trying to exploit a popular genre that she had grown up with the music. She duetted with Boyz II Men on *One Sweet Day* in 1995 and invited rap stars, such as Jay-Z and Snoop Dogg, to guest on a number of singles.

Carey was divorced from Mottola in 1997. After ten years of incessant recording and touring, as well as great commercial success, Carey had a breakdown in 2001; this coincided with unfavorable reviews

for her albums *Rainbow* (1999) and *Glitter*, which accompanied a poorly reviewed film of the same name in 2001.

In the early years of the 21st century, it seemed that Carey's crown had slipped, as she was panned for both her singing and her acting. However, she bounced back in 2005 with the release of *The Emancipation of Mimi* and more recently, was much praised for her role in the award-winning movie *Precious* (2009).

Left: Carey performed *Hero* at the Neighborhood Inaugural Ball for President Obama in January 2009.

Below: With five Grammy awards to her name, Carey is one of the most successful female artists of all time.

Coco Chanel

Born Gabrielle Bonheur Chanel
August 19, 1883
Saumur, France

Died January 10, 1971
Paris, France

'Simplicity,' said fashion designer Coco Chanel, 'is the keynote of all true elegance' and this belief underlined all her designs. Her garments were truly timeless – the famous 'little black dress' is still a staple of many wardrobes 80 years after Coco first devised it – and she introduced classic suits and trousers for women, as well as perfect accessories, to the world of fashion.

Chanel deliberately shrouded her early life in mystery and knocked ten years off her age. However, it seems that her mother died when she was 12 and Chanel was sent to an orphanage, where she learned to sew. It may be that the austere black-and-white habits of the nuns influenced the starkness and simplicity of her later designs.

Chanel acquired the nickname 'Coco' during a short career as a cabaret singer from 1905 to 1908. She worked as a seamstress by day and became the mistress of the textile heir, Etienne Balsan. His patronage enabled her to start designing hats and by 1913, she was able to open her first millinery shop. The financial support of a new lover, Arthur 'Boy' Capel, funded new boutiques in Deauville and Biarritz, the coastal playgrounds of wealthy French people in the pre-war years. Next, Chanel introduced women's sportswear, an entirely new concept, which allowed women to wear practical clothing for outdoor activities.

It was Chanel's move into haute couture from 1918 that revolutionized women's fashion in the first half of the 20th century. The role of women in society had changed during World War I, as they acquired a new independence. Chanel's designs both reflected and encouraged this evolution, replacing the corsets and restrictive clothing of the Victorian era with innovative, elegantly designed clothes. Many of her designs were inspired by menswear and were made up in jersey fabric, which was simple, practical and – best of all for the cash-strapped designer – cheap.

By the mid-1920s, Chanel's reputation as an inspired couturier was well established. Her boutique in Paris's rue Gambon sold simple daywear, classic blazers, suits, sailor tops and straight skirts, as well as lace and tulle evening gowns. She also introduced the signature Chanel No. 5 perfume in 1921, explaining that perfume 'is the unseen, unforgettable, ultimate accessory of fashion ... that heralds your arrival and prolongs your departure.'

Chanel's departure from Paris was itself prolonged after World War II, when public anger at her close wartime relations with a member of the Nazi regime forced her into exile in Switzerland. But she returned in 1954, aged 70 and ignoring the criticism of the fashion press, resumed her place as a style icon. 'Chanel – above all else – is a style,' she once said. 'Fashion, you see, goes out of fashion. Style never.'

Right: 'Luxury must be comfortable, otherwise it is not luxury.' Wise words from the perfectly groomed Coco Chanel, who was always the image of simple elegance.

Below: Chanel (right) with a client, actress Ina Clare, 1931.

Charlie Chaplin

Born Born Charles Spencer
Chaplin
April 16, 1889
London, England

Died December 25, 1977
Vevey, Switzerland

If there is one image that captures the essence of Hollywood, it is Charlie Chaplin's bowler-hatted Little Tramp, the mischievous everyman figure he created in the days of silent movies.

Chaplin was born into poverty in south London and his life encapsulates the sort of rags-to-riches story so popular with movie fans. The son of an alcoholic father and incapable mother, he rose by sheer talent and hard work to become the most acclaimed actor of his generation and one of the best-known movie stars in the world.

Chaplin performed in music hall and vaudeville in London as a child. After touring the United States with the Fred Karno troupe, from 1910 to 1912, he decided to remain there. He quickly got a job with Mack Sennett's Keystone Film Company, although he found it hard to make the move from stage to screen acting. He persevered, though and the Little Tramp made the first of 35 short-film appearances in 1914, in *Kid Auto Races at Venice*. With his trademark baggy suit, bowler hat, mustache and twirling cane, the Little Tramp became the most popular character of the silent movie era, epitomizing the struggle of the underdog against authority.

Chaplin's early work for Keystone relied on physical slapstick for much of its humor. In 1919, in a bid to break out and exert more creative control, he founded the United Artists company with Mary Pickford, Douglas Fairbanks and the film director, D.W. Griffith. He moved from short movies to acting, producing and directing feature-length films: he released *The Kid* in 1921, but only three more, including his masterpiece, *The Gold Rush*

(1925), between 1923 and 1929. Famously a perfectionist, Chaplin re-shot scenes many times, until they were exactly right. He rarely worked from a script, tending to improvise his films around single ideas and allowing the narrative to build gradually.

Chaplin did not let the advent of sound in 1927 alter his film-making technique. He made three more silent movies, *The Circus* (1928), *City Lights* (1931) and *Modern Times* (1936), before his first talkie, *The Great Dictator* (1940), his defiant send-up of Hitler and the Nazis. At the first Academy Awards ceremony in 1929, he was given a Special Award 'for versatility and genius' in producing *The Circus*.

Chaplin did not hide his left-leaning political views and his colorful private life was a poorly kept secret. But in 1952, during the anti-communist era of McCarthyism in the USA, he was accused of 'un-American activities' and spent the rest of his life in Switzerland. He returned to America only once, to receive an honorary Oscar in 1972. Angered by the reaction of his adopted country, Chaplin satirized American

politics and society in his last leading role, in *0* (1957). Nevertheless, he is forever associated with the early days of Hollywood and remains the most respected actor and director of that era.

Left: Chaplin in his iconic role as the Little Tramp, with actor Jackie Coogan in the classic silent movie, *The Kid*.

Below: Charlie Chaplin in a scene from his 1918 film *Shoulder Arms*.

Cher

Born Cherilyn Sarkisian
May 20, 1946
El Centro, California, USA

Remarkable for her long career in the entertainment industry, Cher has survived thanks to her natural talent, sheer hard work and a chameleon-like ability to reinvent herself. As a singer, actress, director and record producer, she has won major awards for her work in films, music and television.

Born in California, Cher began her musical career as a session singer at the age of 17 and began working for record producer, Sonny Bono. The pair quickly formed a highly successful personal and professional partnership, marrying in 1964 and releasing their first smash hit, *I Got You Babe*, in 1965. They projected a psychedelic, soft rock image, with Cher as the wise-cracking, exotically dressed half of the duo and Sonny as the good-natured recipient of her wit. They had a series of hits together, all produced by Sonny, as well as individual solo successes, such as Cher's version of Bob Dylan's *All I Really Want to Do* (1965).

As their record sales declined at the end of the 1960s, Sonny tried (unsuccessfully) to launch their film career, but he had more luck with a series of Las Vegas shows, which paved the way for an immensely successful TV career, notably the *Sonny and Cher Comedy Hour* (1971–4). Meanwhile, Cher continued with her recording career, achieving several No. 1 hits, such as *Gypsys, Tramps & Thieves* (1971) and *Dark Lady* (1974).

Sonny and Cher's marriage disintegrated very publicly in 1975 and Cher's solo career entered a lackluster phase. It was acting, Cher's first love, that relaunched her career in the 1980s and earned her a number of plaudits – from a Golden Globe nomination for *Come Back to the Five and Dime, Jimmy Dean, Jimmy Dean* (1982), to an Oscar for Best Actress in 1988 for her performance as a homely clerk in the romantic comedy, *Moonstruck.* Nominated for Best Supporting Actress for *Silkwood* in 1984, she also starred in the wickedly funny *The Witches of Eastwick,* alongside Jack Nicholson in 1987.

Cher enjoyed another round of musical success from the end of the 1980s, releasing new albums and internationally popular singles. They included *If I Could Turn Back Time* (1989), whose video was banned from MTV, as Cher performed clad in a characteristically flamboyant costume, deemed too revealing for TV audiences. Her 23rd album, *Believe* (1998), produced the biggest hit of her long career, as the title track reached the No. 1 spot in 23 countries around the world. Her elaborate live concerts are legendary, typically including complicated choreography and lavish costumes.

Her personal life has been as colorful as her stage costumes and has contributed to Cher's status as one of the great musical divas, as well as a Hollywood legend.

Right: Demonstrating an uncanny talent for seeking out the limelight, Cher wears a show-stopping costume at the Academy Awards, 1986.

Below: Cher began her career alongside first husband, Sonny Bono, during the 1960s and early 1970s.

Eric Clapton

Born Eric Patrick Clapton
March 30, 1945
Ripley, Surrey, England

Eric Clapton is one of a handful of iconic British musicians who came of age in the 1960s and continued to produce hits for decades after their initial success. The opposite of the one-hit wonder, Clapton is universally admired as one of the most talented guitarists of his generation.

Clapton learned to play guitar as a teenager and developed his love of blues while at art school in Kingston, Surrey. In 1963, he joined the Yardbirds, a rock band with their roots in Clapton's beloved blues music. Just as they had their first hit, *For Your Love*, in 1965, Clapton left, disillusioned with the band's new pop direction. In the meantime, he had forged a reputation as a tremendously skilled instrumentalist, inspiring a well-known piece of 1960s graffiti, 'Clapton is God.' He played with a succession of R&B bands, before forming Cream in 1966, with Jack Bruce and Ginger Baker.

In the two years of the band's existence, Cream assumed the status of a supergroup, winning both critical and commercial success. For Clapton, this was certainly one of the high points of his long career and allowed him to develop his already impressive technical skills, while also lending his singing voice to hits such as *Sunshine of Your Love* (1968) and *Crossroads* (1969). However, Cream soon broke up in a maelstrom of artistic differences, drink and drugs. After a short spell with Blind Faith, Clapton spent a period guesting with other groups, such as the Plastic Ono Band. He was keen to shrug off his own cult status and appeared embarrassed by the extreme adulation of his fans.

Clapton's heroin addiction may have been his way of coping with the stresses of fame, but it came close to killing him and was succeeded by a heavy dependence on alcohol. Yet despite these personal struggles, he produced some unforgettable records, including the poignant *Layla* (1970), his version of Bob Marley's *I Shot the Sheriff* (1974) and *Wonderful Tonight* (1977).

The release of *Money and Cigarettes* in 1983 signaled a new era for a Clapton, free from the problems of drink and drugs. In 1985, he won a BAFTA for his soundtrack for the BBC thriller *Edge of Darkness. Journeyman* (1989) was a collaborative album with George Harrison, Phil Collins and Chaka Khan among others, playing a mixture of blues, pop, jazz and soul.

Clapton continued to play with a variety of his fellow musicians throughout the 1990s, from Roger Waters to Sheryl Crow and B.B. King, both in concert and on albums, such as *From the Cradle. Tears in Heaven*, the moving single Clapton wrote after the death of his four-year-old son, won three Grammy awards in 1992.

Frequently cited as one of the most influential guitarists of all time, Clapton is one of rock's great survivors.

Above: A regular performer at charity concerts, Clapton performs alongside Jeff Beck and Jimmy Page.

Left: Clapton performs at a reunion of Cream at Madison Square Garden, 2005.

Kurt Cobain

Born Kurt Donald Cobain
February 20, 1967
Aberdeen, Washington,
USA

Died Died April 5, 1994
Seattle, Washington, USA

Musician and songwriter Kurt Cobain's early death, at the age of 27, ensured his immortality as one of the most significant rock stars of the 1990s.

Heavily influenced by punk and the alternative music of underground and indie groups, Cobain's band, Nirvana, became America's premier grunge group, combining a stadium rock feel with abrasive lyrics. Their hit *Smells like Teen Spirit* (1991) became the anthem of a generation, who cast Cobain as their spokesman.

Kurt Cobain was born and grew up in a small town, 140 miles south of Seattle. His parents divorced when he was seven, leaving him with feelings of insecurity and anguish that were later to show in Nirvana's music. Given a guitar when he was 14, he taught himself to play and gradually began writing his own songs.

After a false start with his first band, the attractively named Fecal Matter, Cobain formed Nirvana with bass player Krist Novoselic in 1987. They immediately began touring the Seattle area, making little impact. However, their first album, *Bleach*, released in 1989, received a lot of airplay on college radio stations and established the band on the indie scene.

Cobain reveled in the alternative, underground rock roots of Nirvana. He struggled to reconcile his natural dislike of corporate big business with his desire for popular and commercial success. But swallowing their principles in order to get the punk message to a wider audience, Nirvana signed with DGC Records to release their breakthrough album *Nevermind* in 1991. *Nevermind* certainly fulfilled the band's ambitions, eventually selling 10 million copies in the USA alone and knocking Michael Jackson's *Dangerous* from the No. 1 spot.

The album's first single, *Smells like Teen Spirit*, was swiftly followed by *Come as You Are* and in the first months of 1992, Nirvana became a global phenomenon. Their mainstream success came with all the usual fuss from the media, particularly when Cobain married fellow musician Courtney Love in Hawaii, a few months before their daughter was born. But by the end of that year, despite the personal happiness he had found with his new family, drugs had taken over in Cobain's life. He struggled with a heroin habit from 1991 until the end of his life, overdosing several times.

In 1993, Nirvana's third album, *In Utero*, which *Rolling Stone* magazine described as 'brilliant, corrosive, enraged and thoughtful,' shot into the charts at No. 1. The band embarked on a US tour and then went to Europe in early 1994 – a tour that was cut short on March 4 by Cobain's overdose. He admitted himself to rehab, but committed suicide on April 5, 1994. Kurt Cobain's death provoked shock, anger and grief from his fans and true regret from critics, who admired his angry, thought-provoking music and lyrics.

Right: 'It's better to burn out than fade away,' said Kurt Cobain in 1993.

Below: Cobain crowd surfs in his home town of Seattle, Washington, 1990.

Sir Sean Connery

Born Thomas Sean Connery
August 25, 1930
Edinburgh, Scotland

One of Scotland's biggest film stars, Connery most famously made the role of James Bond his own in seven hugely successful and trendsetting films, between 1962 and 1983. His later career, as a much-loved Hollywood professional, has seen him making box office hits well into his seventies.

Legend has it, that Connery was working as a milk delivery man when he landed the role of Bond. In fact, he had played his first stage and film roles in the 1950s and co-starred with Claire Bloom in a TV version of *Anna Karenina* in 1961.

But it was his gritty, sensual, predatory Bond that established not only his own career, but an enduring film character. Author Ian Fleming's creation was a cold-blooded, daring, but rather two-dimensional womanizer; Connery added substance and a sense of humor. The early films, such as *Dr. No* (1962) and *Thunderball* (1965), were genuinely suspenseful and for the time, risqué. Fleming, initially unsure whether Connery was the right man for the role, gave Bond a half-Scottish, half-Swiss background in his later novels, in tribute to the actor.

Connery's later outings in the role, such as *Diamonds Are Forever* (1971), became slightly self-parodying and the films themselves were increasingly spectacular, gadget-oriented and improbably plotted. He had other successful roles while making the Bond films, notably in Alfred Hitchcock's *Marnie* (1964), John Huston's *The Man Who Would Be King* (1975) and Terry Gilliam's *Time Bandits* (1981).

A thoughtful and serious actor, who prepared carefully for his roles, Connery never allowed himself to be typecast and had a series of big hits in the 1980s. These include the popular fantasy *Highlander*, the historical thriller *The Name of the Rose* (both 1986), de Palma's *The Untouchables* (1987), which won him his only Oscar for his crafty Irish cop and *Indiana Jones and the Last Crusade* (1989), in which he played Harrison Ford's father. More recent successes have included roles as an ageing cat burglar in *Entrapment* (1999), a reclusive author in *Finding Forrester* (2000) and a Victorian version of Bond in *The League of Extraordinary Gentlemen* (2003). The last was an unhappy experience, which appears to have hastened his retirement.

In 1989, Connery was voted the Sexiest Man Alive by the US weekly *People* magazine, but official recognition of his services both to film and to British exports was slow to come. His active support for the Scottish National Party, which campaigns for Scottish independence from the UK, is thought to have delayed for many years his long-awaited knighthood, but it finally came in 2000. A major philanthropist, Connery donated his entire salary from *Diamonds Are Forever* – well over $1million – to the Scottish Educational Trust, which he co-founded.

Left: Connery in his most famous role, as James Bond in the first Bond movie, *Dr No.*

Below: In 1989 Connery appeared as Professor Henry Jones, father of Indiana Jones, in *Indiana Jones and the Last Crusade.*

Marie Curie

Born Marya Skłodowska
November 7, 1867
Warsaw, Poland

Died July 4, 1934
Passy, France

The Polish-born chemist, Marie Curie, is one of the best-known scientists of her day. Together with her husband, Pierre, she carried out pioneering work in the field of radioactivity (a term she coined) and she was the first person ever to win the Nobel Prize twice.

Marya was the child of teachers in Warsaw, whose families had suffered financial hardship through their support for Polish independence. She began her scientific studies in Warsaw, having first worked as a governess to support herself and then transferred to the University of the Sorbonne, in Paris, in 1891. There she gained degrees in both physics and mathematics, changed her name to Marie and met the Frenchman, Pierre Curie, who was a professor in the School of Physics. They married in 1895 and set up a shared laboratory.

The Curies jointly investigated the nature of radioactivity, building on the research of Marie's older colleague, Henri Becquerel, into the radioactive element, uranium. But it was Marie alone, using the electrometer (which measured electrical charge) invented by her husband, who discovered that uranium emitted radiation by itself and not as a result of interaction with other molecules. She went on to observe that one particular uranium ore emitted much larger amounts of radiation, suggesting to her the existence

of a new element. In July 1898, she and Pierre announced that they had discovered polonium and followed this up in December with the announcement of another element, radium.

The Curies received the Nobel Prize for Physics in 1903, for their work on radioactivity, jointly with Becquerel. Marie then worked to isolate radium in appreciable quantities. She continued to work alone after her husband was killed in 1906 in a street accident. In 1911, she was awarded the Nobel Prize for Chemistry for their joint discovery of radium and polonium and for her work on the nature and applications of radium.

World War I provided a grim opportunity to demonstrate the value of the Curies' work. Their research lay behind the vital development of x-rays and Marie campaigned for mobile radiography units, using radium tubes derived from her work to treat the wounded. These became known as 'petites curies'.

As well as her huge contribution to science, Curie was a pioneer in the way she overcame a succession of hurdles placed in her way, because she was a woman. She was the first female teacher at the Sorbonne and after her second Nobel Prize win, she persuaded the French government to fund a Radium Institute, now the Institut Curie. This produced four more Nobel Prize winners, including her daughter Irène Joliot-Curie and son-in-law Frédéric Joliot, who were the first people to produce radioactivity artificially. Marie died of leukemia, caused by her exposure to radiation, the dangers of which were then unknown.

Left: Marie Curie in her laboratory, 1905, two years after winning the Nobel Prize for Physics.

Above: Marie and Pierre Curie formed a remarkable partnership, devoting their lives to their research.

51

Salvador Dalí

Born Salvador Domingo Felipe
Jacinto Dalí i Domènech
November 29, 1904
Figueres, Catalonia, Spain

Died January 23, 1989
Figueres, Catalonia, Spain

The Spanish surrealist painter, Salvador Dalí, with his trademark moustache, was one of the most famous – and notorious – artists of the 20th century.

Dalí was an eccentric from his earliest days. He spent long childhood hours in a full washtub in the family laundry room, lost in his own imagination. As an adult, he courted attention with a carefully cultivated public persona, once arriving at a function in a Rolls-Royce filled with cauliflowers.

This flamboyant exhibitionism was, he claimed, the source of his creative energies. A naturally skilled draftsman, he painted constantly from his early teens onwards, initially in an Impressionist style, but soon introducing the exuberant color of Fauvist painters, such as Matisse. In 1921, he enrolled at the Madrid School of Fine Arts, where his friends included the film-maker Luis Buñuel and writer Federico García Lorca. Here he learned the meticulous, academic technique that, with his use of color, was to become one of the characteristics of his work. His first one-man show, in 1925, was admired by his fellow-artists, Picasso and Miró.

But it was Dalí's encounter with Surrealism, until then mainly a literary movement, that gave his work its hallucinatory quality and the style for which he is best known: he used everyday images as a means of accessing the subconscious. The result was a major group of paintings in 1929, including two of his most significant works, *The Enigma of Desire* and *The Great Masturbator*. He also developed his theory of the double, or triple image, in which unrelated objects merge and become parts of a whole. So, in *The Phantom Cart* (1933), the driver seems to metamorphose into a tower and in *Mae West* (1934), the star's face is also an almost unfurnished room.

When Dalí's work was introduced to the US, it caused a sensation. His New York exhibition in 1934 included one of his most famous works, *The Persistence of Memory*, with its surreal image of soft, melting watches. In 1940, Civil war in Spain led Dalí to move to the US and a new period of creative activity followed, in which he applied the discoveries of physics to his existing imagery, in works such as *Atomic Leda* (1949) and *Raphaelesque Head Exploding* (1951). He also threw himself into the celebrity lifestyle, designing jewelry and stage sets, painting society portraits and working with movie director Alfred Hitchcock in Hollywood.

In later years, Dalí reverted to Catholicism and began to work with religious subject-matter. He spent the last 40 years of his life back in the Spanish region of Catalonia, where he continued to experiment with novel media – he was one of the first to exploit the artistic potential of holography. He died at the age of 84 in Figueres, the town of his birth, where the fittingly flamboyant Dalí Museum was built to house many of his works.

Right: Dali with French singer Amanda Lear at his home in Port Lligat, Spain, 1974. Flamboyant, publicity seeking and extremely astute, Dali cultivated an eccentric image, once saying, 'There is only one difference between a madman and me. I am not mad.'

Robert De Niro

Born Robert Mario de Niro Jr.
August 17, 1943
New York City, USA

One of the greatest actors of his time, De Niro made his name in films of often brutal violence, or playing borderline psychotics.

The child of artist parents, the part-Italian De Niro discovered his passion for acting when playing the Cowardly Lion in a school production of *The Wizard of Oz*. He studied acting in New York under Lee Strasberg, chief proponent of Method acting, in which actors create convincing performances by generating the thoughts and emotions of their character within themselves. De Niro's first role was in Brian De Palma's comedy *The Wedding Party*, which was made in 1963, but only released in 1969.

It was De Palma who introduced De Niro to movie director, Martin Scorsese. *Mean Streets* (1973) launched De Niro in his guise as a ferocious, unpredictable force of nature, as the wired and terrifying Johnny Boy, alongside Harvey Keitel's Charlie. The two actors have remained good friends ever since.

This was the start of an extraordinarily fruitful partnership with Martin Scorsese and lead roles in a series of electrifying movies, including *Taxi Driver* (1976), *Raging Bull* (1980) and *Goodfellas* (1990). In *Taxi Driver* – perhaps his most famous collaboration with Scorsese – De Niro played the simmering antihero, Travis Bickle, which established him as a star. To prepare for the part, he worked as a cab driver for some months. The musical *New York, New York* (1977) was a departure for both actor and director, with De Niro as the classic leading man, all good looks and charm. But *Raging Bull* returned him to type, in a role for which he put on 30 kilos

(70 pounds) for the later scenes and trained as a boxer for a year. He won two of the three fights he entered, plus a Best Actor Oscar for the role.

Other classic parts included the young Don Vito Corleone in Francis Ford Coppola's *The Godfather, Part II* (1974), for which De Niro mastered a Sicilian dialect and won his first Oscar, for Best Supporting Actor. But he has also ranged way beyond his mafia roles, starring as the deluded and chilling comedian Pupkin in Scorsese's under-rated *The King of Comedy* (1983) and in comedies such as *Brazil* (1985), *Analyze This* (1999), where he spoofs his mafia persona and *Meet the Parents* (2000) and *Meet the Fockers* (2004) with Ben Stiller.

Over the last 20 years, De Niro has also moved into production and heads his

own company, Tribeca. He made his debut as a director with *A Bronx Tale* in 1993 and had a huge success in 2006 with *The Good Shepherd*, starring Matt Damon and Angelina Jolie, about the origins of the CIA.

Right: De Niro on the set of *The Deer Hunter*, 1978. A seering study of the Vietnam war, the movie won the Academy Award for Best Picture, while De Niro was nominated for Best Actor and still claims that it was the most exhausting film of his career.

Below: Filming the 2004 horror movie *Godsend*.

Overleaf: De Niro in one of his most famous films, *Raging Bull*.

James Dean

Angry, vulnerable and disenchanted, James Dean seemed to epitomize the anguish of youth, both for his own and succeeding generations.

Dean's film career lasted less than five years, from January 1951, when he dropped out of university to be an actor, to September 1955 when he was killed in a car crash. And yet in that brief period and in just three roles, he earned his place in the Hollywood constellation of stars, above all with his most celebrated film, *Rebel Without a Cause* (1955). His early death raised him to icon status, as the rebel who died too young.

Raised on a farm in Indiana, Dean moved to California in 1949 and studied drama, before quitting for a series of movie bit-parts. Determined to make his mark, he joined the legendary Actors' Studio in New York, studying Method acting with Lee Strasberg. A variety of television and stage roles followed and then in 1953, he was picked by director Elia Kazan to play the edgy adolescent Cal Trask in Kazan's movie version (released in 1955) of John Steinbeck's novel *East of Eden*. It is an emotionally complex role: Cal rebels against his puritan father in a classic inter-generational conflict and then discovers that his supposedly dead mother is actually running a nearby brothel.

Dean received a posthumous Best Actor nomination for his role at the 1956 Academy Awards.

But it is for Dean's more central – though just as conflicted – role in Nicholas Ray's *Rebel Without a Cause* that his memory remains eternally fresh. Ray's movie highlights parental failure and troubled youth. At the start, its young hero, Jim, is being held in a police station for public drunkenness. Antagonized by his middle-class parents' mutual hostility and lack of moral strength, he shouts, 'You're tearing me apart' at them. Today it seems a classic teenage tribulation – Jim meets a girl (played by Natalie Wood), becomes mentor to a boy even more confused than himself, falls foul of a gang of bullies and fails to save his friend from dying in a car crash. But in the mid-1950s, it was stunningly new, billing its hero as 'The bad boy from a good family!' The film opened just a month after Dean's own fatal crash: with tragic irony, he was on his way, in his Porsche, to take part in a sports car race – racing being his other passion.

His third film was the sprawling family saga *Giant* (1956), in which, determined not to get typecast, he played an oil-rich Texan, in a support role to Rock Hudson and Elizabeth Taylor. This, too, was nominated for a posthumous Academy Award. But *Rebel Without a Cause* is James Dean's true memorial.

Born	James Byron Dean February 8, 1931 Marion, Indiana, USA
Died	September 30, 1955 Cholame, California, USA

Below: 'Dream as if you'll live forever. Live as if you'll die tomorrow' – poignant words from the young actor, whose career began barely five years before his death in a car crash, aged just 24. Dean is pictured here as Jett Rink, the Texan oil heir, in his last film, *Giant*.

Johnny Depp

Born John Christopher Depp II
June 9, 1963
Owensboro, Kentucky,
USA

Swashbuckling, unconventional and sometimes shocking, Johnny Depp's film roles have been anything but predictable. He has largely avoided blockbusters and brings a benign, humorous, almost mystical aura to all his parts.

Depp's first passion was the guitar. He dropped out of school in 1979 to become a rock musician (he made a solo album in 1997), only later deciding on acting as a career. He made his debut in Wes Craven's creepy, but well-made *A Nightmare on Elm Street* (1984), perhaps a significant precedent for some of the roles that ensued. A number of minor roles followed, but it was the charmingly bizarre *Edward Scissorhands* (1990), his first film with director Tim Burton, which gave him his first real chance to shine. He brought a sense of outcast pathos to a role, that in other hands, might have descended into kitsch.

The relationship with Burton has proved a formative one for them both. They have made seven films together, of which the next was *Ed Wood* (1994), the wacky and unusual story of a film director notorious for writing and directing some of the worst films ever made. *Sleepy Hollow* (1999) was a gothic ghost story in which Depp played detective Ichabod Crane as a delicate, feminine character, at odds with the wild events the film portrays.

Willie Wonka, in *Charlie and the Chocolate Factory* (2005), based on the book by Roald Dahl, was another Burton character created by Depp, while his much praised performance as the titular character in *Sweeney Todd: The Demon Barber of Fleet Street* (2007), based on the Stephen Sondheim musical, gave him his first chance to sing and won him an Oscar

nomination for Best Actor. A more recent outing in a Tim Burton movie was the Mad Hatter in *Alice in Wonderland* (2010), which set a new box office record for its opening day's takings.

Beyond his work with Burton, Depp has continued to make interesting and offbeat choices. In a two-year period from 1997 to 1999, he starred in Mike Newell's gangster movie *Donnie Brasco*, Terry Gilliam's *Fear and Loathing in Las Vegas*, the sci-fi shocker *The Astronaut's Wife* and Roman Polanski's tale of decadence among the very rich, *The Ninth Gate*. But perhaps his most iconic role and the one that has cemented his star status, is as Captain Jack Sparrow in the *Pirates of the Caribbean* movies. The first of these was slow to take off at the box office, but the second, *Pirates of the Caribbean: Dead Man's Chest* (2006), grossed a record-making $136 million in its first three days.

Depp himself says that he has a lot in common with Sparrow. In 2007, in gratitude to a London hospital for the care his daughter received there when her kidneys failed, he spent a half day in the children's ward in his Jack Sparrow costume.

Left: Mercurial, unpredictable and always interesting, Johnny Depp has made his name by portraying off-beat, charismatic characters.

Below: As Captain Jack Sparrow from the immensely successful *Pirates of the Caribbean* movies.

Overleaf: Depp arrives at the Venice Film Festival, 2007.

Diana, Princess of Wales

Diana Spencer became, for a time, the most famous woman in the world after her fairytale wedding, in 1981, to the Prince of Wales, heir to the British throne.

The subject of numerous biographies and gossip features, both during and after her scandal-strewn marriage and after her controversial death, Diana remains the pre-eminent female celebrity of her generation. People's princess, English rose, charity campaigner, fashion icon, tragic victim: Diana was all these and an unwitting force for change in the world of the British monarchy.

Diana was born into an aristocratic English family, the granddaughter of the 7th Earl Spencer and became Lady Diana Spencer when her father inherited the title in 1975. Her engagement and marriage were greeted with delight and the wedding in St Paul's Cathedral was watched by an estimated 750 million television viewers worldwide.

Diana was a devoted and hands-on mother to her sons, Princes William and Harry, born in 1982 and 1984 – she fitted her public duties round her children's schedules, in a manner novel to the British royal family. However, she felt stifled and unsupported within the royal entourage. Even before her wedding, she was showing signs of stress and her battle with bulimia continued through much of her marriage.

In the 1990s, that marriage became the subject of feverish public speculation. Both parties used the media to put their case, in a way that permanently altered the relations between British royalty and the press. Stories of Diana's 'hysterical' accusations and suicide attempts were balanced by her increasingly confident and glamorous public persona. Initially demure and traditional, her style developed into that of an international celebrity. Her appearance was carefully considered. She was always able to look right for the occasion, whether wearing waterproofs on deck, Chanel on a state visit to Paris, or a stunning ink-blue creation to dance with John Travolta at the White House.

As her private life crumbled, Diana threw her energies into her increasingly significant charitable work, notably against the use of landmines and for victims of AIDS, at a time when there was huge social stigma attached to the disease. After her separation (1992) and divorce (1996) from Prince Charles, she ceased to be Her Royal Highness, the Princess of Wales and instead used the title Diana, Princess of Wales. But to the world's media, she remained Princess Di, newsworthy as ever, as they chronicled her increasingly close relationship with Dodi Al-Fayed, playboy son of the owner of Harrods department store in London. Their death together in a car crash in Paris, still the subject of wild conspiracy theories, was probably caused by their driver's attempts to avoid the paparazzi. The extraordinary outpouring of public grief that followed was ample testament to Diana's power to touch hearts worldwide.

Born Diana Frances Spencer
July 1, 1961
Sandringham, Norfolk, England

Died August 31, 1997
Paris, France

Right: 'The People's Princess,' as Diana was dubbed, pictured in October, 1995.

Below: Diana's wedding day, 1981.

Walt Disney

Animator supreme and creator of Mickey Mouse, Dumbo and Snow White, Walt Disney was a risk-taker and genuine innovator, as well as an inspired businessman. Though the Walt Disney Company was blamed by many commentators over the years for the increased uniformity and globalization of the movie world, Walt's mission to bring a little fantasy into people's lives is still pursued on a mammoth scale by the company he founded.

Disney's first company, Laugh-O-Gram Films, was founded with commercial artist Ub Iwerks in 1922 to make short animations. Walt's financier brother, Roy, joined them in 1923, when they moved to Los Angeles and established their own studio. After one disaster, when a deal fell through and they failed to retain the rights in their own creation, Walt reputedly came up with the Oscar-winning idea of Mickey Mouse on the train ride. Though he was drawn by the more gifted Ub, Mickey's radical contribution to animation, at Walt's insistence, was synchronized sound – he voiced the character himself. Two years later, Roy made an equally important contribution to the history of Disney, by signing a licensing deal to manufacture Mickey Mouse products.

Snow White and the Seven Dwarfs (1937), their major breakthrough, was America's first ever feature-length animation. The Disney Company went into serious debt to fund it, but it made a staggering $8 million on its release and won another Oscar, encouraging Walt to make the long, ambitious *Fantasia* (1940). This was intended to raise animation to an art form and also won an Oscar, but was dismissed by critics as kitsch and tasteless and made a loss. Despite *Bambi* and *Dumbo* (both 1942), the company continued to struggle and *Cinderella* (1950) was a money-making exercise.

Disney decided that the answer was to diversify. In 1950, he moved into live-action features, with the well-received *Treasure Island* and a series of good-looking natural history documentaries. The *Walt Disney* program first appeared on television in 1954 and ran profitably for over 30 years. In 1955, Walt opened the first theme park, Disneyland, in California. But he is perhaps best remembered for the delightful *Mary Poppins* (1964): with its innovative mix of live action and animation, it was a very personal project, which he worked hard to bring to the screen. Julie Andrews won an Oscar for the title role.

After Disney's death two years later, the company, then the world's leading producer of family entertainment, languished for a while. But in the 1980s, under lively new management, it saw a return to form – particularly under the Touchstone Pictures banner – with

Born Walter Elias Disney
December 5, 1901
Chicago, Illinois, USA

Died December 15, 1966
Burbank, California, USA

successes as varied as *Who Framed Roger Rabbit* (1988), *Dead Poets Society* (1989) and *Pretty Woman* (1990). A series of classic animations in the 1990s included *Aladdin* (1992) and *The Lion King* (1994), while the collaboration with Pixar that produced *Toy Story* (1995) and *Finding Nemo* (2003) brought Disney into the age of computer animation.

Left: 'If you can dream it, you can do it. Always remember that this whole thing was started with a dream and a mouse,' said Disney, pictured here with Mickey, 1935.

Right: Avuncular animator Walt Disney combined a consummate popular touch with canny business skills and a genuine desire to entertain the world.

Bob Dylan

Born Robert Allen Zimmerman
May 24, 1941
Duluth, Minnesota, USA

Evergreen and inscrutable, the hugely influential American singer-songwriter and rock musician, Bob Dylan, is one of the greats of the 20th century. He has been performing and touring for over 50 years.

Dylan first became an inspirational figure with his 1960s protest songs and the powerful lyrics of numbers such as *Blowin' in the Wind* and *The Times They Are a-Changin'* became anthems for the anti-war and civil rights movements of that era. His strong melodies and increasingly sophisticated lyrics came for a while to define the folk genre.

As a boy, Bob Dylan was influenced by contemporary blues, country and early rock and roll and his first albums were largely covers of existing folk, blues and gospel music. His first protest songs were in the melancholy style of his musical hero, Woody Guthrie, but he soon gained his own political and musical voice, notably on the 1964 album *The Times They Are a-Changin'.* His raw presentation of his own material was not to every taste, however and many of his early songs were initially hits for other people – *Blowin' in the Wind* for Peter, Paul and Mary in 1963 and *Mr. Tambourine Man* for The Byrds in 1965.

In 1965, Dylan shocked his more purist folk audience by choosing to perform with an electric rock band and was booed at the Newport Folk Festival. However, the intensity of his performance and the subtlety of the lyrics on his albums *Highway 61 Revisited* and *Blonde on Blonde*, reinforced by indecipherable and contradictory interviews, brought him celebrity status. The electric band (known simply as The Band) became a

permanent Dylan feature. The rock world was revolutionized by Dylan's new sound, a synthesis of his own varied styles with an overlay of British rock (Dylan and The Beatles met and worked together in 1964).

Dylan was showered with honors throughout the 1970s and 1980s – he was inducted into the Rock and Roll Hall of Fame in 1989 and given a Grammy Lifetime Achievement Award in 1991. His albums of the period were perhaps of variable quality. In 1988, however, he embarked on what became known as 'The Never-Ending Tour,' a constant stream of live shows that continues to pull in capacity audiences. *Time Out of Mind* (1997), his first album of original material

for seven years, received his strongest reviews for years and three Grammy awards. In 2004, he was rated second in *Rolling Stone* magazine's 'Greatest Artists of All Time,' stimulating a revival of interest in his music which was reinforced by the success of *Modern Times* (2006).

Academic critics have drawn attention to the cultural richness of Dylan's influences, literary as well as musical. In 2008, this was recognized with the award of a special Pulitzer citation for his profound impact on popular music and American culture.

Left: Dylan in concert, 1980.

Below: A young Bob with folk singer Joan Baez in 1965.

Clint Eastwood

Born Clinton Eastwood Jr.
May 31, 1930
San Francisco, California,
USA

Hollywood legend, Clint Eastwood, boasts two brilliant and overlapping careers, as a much-lauded film actor and as a successful director and producer.

He made his name, ironically, as the macho 'Man with No Name' in Sergio Leone's 1960s spaghetti westerns and then in a series of loner roles for Don Siegel. In 1970, he formed his own film company, Malpaso and since then has directed many films, alternating mainstream thrillers with more personal projects.

Born during the Great Depression, Eastwood worked as a lumberjack and served in the army, before being signed to Universal for a series of small parts in the 1950s. His role in the television series *Rawhide* (1959–66) brought him to Leone's attention. *A Fistful of Dollars* (1964), low-budget and shot in three months, redefined (with its two follow-ups, *For a Few Dollars More* and *The Good, the Bad and the Ugly*) both the western and its stereotypical hero. Eastwood was launched. Later, his fruitful partnership with Don Siegel saw him exchanging arbitrary brutality for a more thoughtful approach to what is portrayed as a naturally violent world. In *Dirty Harry* (1971), he gives a tough, but sympathetic portrayal of a cop driven by disorder and inept bureaucracy to take the law into his own hands.

The first film that Eastwood both directed and starred in was a significant choice. A thriller, *Play Misty for Me* (1971) is an intriguing story of male assurance destroyed by female paranoia – in effect, Eastwood sending up Eastwood. As a producer, he has developed a tight-knit team of collaborators, keeps a firm hand on budgets and shoots his movies with exemplary speed. Many of them, though not necessarily lauded by the critics, have continued to mine the reliable western and *Dirty Harry* veins, as in *High Plains Drifter* (1973), *The Gauntlet* (1977) and *The Rookie* (1990).

At the same time, he has made a sequence of diverse and much less predictable films. Some of these, such as the tough, but lyrical *The Outlaw Josey Wales* (1976), the bleak western *The Unforgiven* (1992) and the highly acclaimed thriller *Mystic River* (2003), continued to take violence as their main theme. But there were also delicately handled romances, notably *The Bridges of Madison County* (1995), which starred Eastwood in an improbable, but popular pairing with Meryl Streep. *Honkytonk Man* (1982) is a character piece, with Eastwood playing an ageing and alcoholic country singer, while the touching and well-observed *Million Dollar Baby* (2004), with Hilary Swank as the wannabe boxer and Clint as her reluctant trainer, won four Oscars.

With his pair of double-perspective World War II films, *Flags of Our Fathers* and *Letters from Iwo Jima* (2006), Eastwood proved beyond doubt that he is at the peak of his game, still making powerful and individual films in his seventies.

Right: Tough, loner roles in spaghetti westerns established Eastwood's career in the early 1960s, when he became famous for his inscrutable screen presence.

Right: Eastwood as Harry Callahan in the first *Dirty Harry* film.

Overleaf: *The Good, the Bad and the Ugly*, 1966.

Albert Einstein

Born March 14, 1879
Ulm, Württemberg,
Germany

Died April 18, 1955
Princeton, New Jersey,
USA

Einstein stands alongside Galileo and Isaac Newton, as one of a handful of scientific thinkers, who have redefined our understanding of the universe. The German-born theoretical physicist and philosopher founded the concept of the 'space-time continuum' and is often described as the father of modern physics.

However, in his youth, Einstein's genius was not obvious. He struggled first to qualify for higher education and then to find a teaching post. While continuing to study, he finally landed a job in 1902 at the Swiss patent office – having already become a Swiss national – evaluating applications for electromagnetic devices.

In 1905, aged only 26, Einstein published four research papers, which came to be recognized as revolutionary in content and are known as the *Annus Mirabilis Papers.* Stimulated by apparent inconsistencies within current atomic and light-wave theory to take a new approach, Einstein sought to formulate new principles that might offer an underlying context for these puzzling phenomena, while remaining consistent with the established laws of physics. This new methodology has become the standard tool which defines modern theoretical physics.

His first new principle was that of special relativity, introduced in a paper on the electrodynamics of moving bodies, which postulated that the speed of light remains absolute, irrespective of the movement of the observer. He argued that as bodies approach the speed of light, they become shorter and heavier; this, in turn, led him to the view that energy (E) and mass (m) are two different aspects of the same thing. The resulting equation relating the two, $E = mc^2$, which many can cite, but few can explain, laid the basis for harnessing nuclear energy and the invention of the atom bomb.

Einstein's papers were so radical, that their significance was not immediately recognized. It was four more years before he was given a university post, a professorship at Zurich in 1909. In 1915, he generalized the theory of relativity to show its connection with gravitation, treating the gravitational force experienced by a body as a property of space and time, which he suggested was 'curved' by the presence of mass. The path of light and the motion of planets and stars are dictated by this curvature of space in the neighborhood of matter.

In 1919, when experimental data verified this theory, Einstein's name was finally made and in 1921, he received the Nobel Prize for Physics. He was lecturing in California when Hitler came to power in Germany in 1933 and as a Jew, wisely decided to stay in the USA. He became a US citizen and spent the rest of his life at the Institute for Advanced Study at Princeton, trying to formulate a unified field theory, a goal that still eludes physicists today. A pacifist, he was an active postwar supporter of nuclear disarmament, recognizing that the nuclear age had been launched by his theory of relativity.

Left and below: Einstein was arguably the best known scientist of the 20th century and his name is now a byword for exceptional intelligence.

Harrison Ford

Born July 13, 1942
Chicago, Illinois, USA

The ultimate rugged American box office draw, star of two of the most successful movie franchises of all time, the highest earning Hollywood actor ever – the superlatives come thick and fast where Harrison Ford is concerned.

However, Ford's career started slowly. Determined on an acting profession as soon as he left college, he moved to Los Angeles in 1964 to apply for a radio voice-over job. He played a number of bit-parts in film and television during the 1960s and early 1970s, including roles in *Ironside* and *The Virginian*, but became disenchanted with his progress and taught himself carpentry to support his young family.

In 1973, George Lucas cast him in a support role to Richard Dreyfuss in *American Graffiti*, but although the movie made Lucas's name, it still did not kick-start Ford's career. He played a couple of parts for Francis Ford Coppola, but was still doing his carpentry when, in 1975, Lucas asked him to read for a new project and finally cast him as Han Solo in the epoch-making sci-fi epic *Star Wars* (1977). Lucas himself said that he intended the movie, a classic struggle between good and evil, for a generation growing up without fairy tales and Ford's detached, but ultimately heroic character provided a welcome note of moral ambivalence.

Star Wars led to two follow-ups and also to Ford's next major outing, this time with the other great originator of movie blockbusters, Steven Spielberg. As Indiana Jones, in the riotous adventure escapade *Raiders of the Lost Ark* (1981), Ford reveled both in the intense action

sequences – he performed many of his own stunts – and in the knockabout humor. This, too, led to more films – *Indiana Jones and the Temple of Doom* (1984), *Indiana Jones and the Last Crusade* (1988), and *Indiana Jones and the Kingdom of the Crystal Skull* (2008).

After his first Indiana Jones outing, Ford's next major film, the bleak, futuristic *Blade Runner* (1982), was another gritty sci-fi style role. Any risk of typecasting was avoided by *Witness* (1985), in which his detective character joins an Amish community to protect a child witness to murder. The movie proved a sensitive exploration of different cultures and gained Ford an Oscar nomination. He reprised his portrayal of the troubled guy under abnormal pressure in *Presumed Innocent* (1990) and *The Fugitive* (1993), made his first romantic comedy with Melanie Griffith in *Working Girl* (1988) and subverted his own heroic image in the supernatural thriller *What Lies Beneath* (2000).

Ford returned to action movies in *Patriot Games* (1992), with Sean Bean and in *Air Force One* (1997), as the heroic US President saving the day. In 1997, he was ranked first in *Empire's list of* 'Top 100 Movie Stars of All Time'.

Having proved his versatility and starred in four of the ten top-grossing movies of all time, Ford has become choosier about his roles in the 21st century. He carefully guards his private life with his long-term girlfriend, the actress Calista Flockhart.

Above and overleaf: As Rick Deckard in Ridley Scott's *Blade Runner*, which Ford has called 'not one of my favorite films.'

Right: Ford's archetypal role, as gung-ho archeologist Indiana Jones, has made him the highest-earning Hollywood actor of all time.

Michael J. Fox

Born Michael Andrew Fox
June 9, 1961
Abbotsford, British
Columbia, Canada

Actor, voice-over artist and campaigner, Michael J. Fox is known above all for two long-running sitcoms, for his starring role in the *Back to the Future* trilogy and for his courageous revelation, in 1998, that he had been diagnosed with Parkinson's disease seven years earlier.

The son of a career soldier, during his childhood, Fox moved frequently around Canada with his family. His charmingly boyish face landed him his first acting job, playing a ten-year-old, when aged 15, in the CBC series *Leo and Me* (1976).

Roles in regional theater followed and in 1979, Fox dropped out of school and moved to Los Angeles. At first, he struggled and was all set to call it a day, when in 1981, he got the part of the aspiring, conservative, self-serving teenager, Alex P. Keaton, on the NBC sitcom *Family Ties* (1982–9). This won him three Emmy awards and made him one of the biggest stars of the 1980s, embodying the culture clash of the Reagan era in Alex's relations with his laid-back, liberal parents. The role was a defining one in a personal sense, too, as Michael met his future wife, Tracy Pollan, on set.

His effortless comic timing and classic 'boy-next-door' good looks earned him the part of time-traveling, guitar-playing Marty McFly in Steven Spielberg's hugely successful, light-hearted fantasy *Back to the Future* (1985). Unfortunately, this had the effect of typecasting him. He made a number of movies in the late 1980s in an effort to change career direction, but none of them won him the same acclaim. His most successful role was as a humane and horrified GI to Sean Penn's tough and depraved sergeant in Brian De Palma's bleak Vietnam War saga *Casualties of War*

(1989). His return in *Back to the Future 2* and *3* (1989 and 1990, shot back-to-back) was welcomed both by critics and the movie-going public and he added a new talent to his portfolio when he provided the narration for the Disney animal adventure remake *Homeward Bound: The Incredible Journey* (1993). More rewarding parts followed and in 1996, Fox signed for another sitcom, *Spin City*, as a fast-talking New York mayoral aide.

After announcing his diagnosis, Fox has continued to make public appearances, despite the shakes and tremors that are symptoms of Parkinson's, as part of his campaigning support for federally funded stem-cell research. He has also carried on acting, both doing voice-overs and taking

parts that reflect his own disabilities: he won an Emmy nomination for his four-episode role as a lung cancer patient in the television series *Boston Legal* and an Emmy award in 2009, for his abrasive paraplegic in the series *Rescue Me*. He founded the Michael J. Fox Foundation in 2000 to aid all avenues of research into the causes and treatment of neurological disorders.

Left: As Marty McFly, the time-traveling teenager in the *Back to the Future* movies.

Above: Fox's courageous struggle with Parkinson's disease, away from the silver screen, has earned him worldwide respect.

Aretha Franklin

Born Aretha Louise Franklin
March 25, 1942
Memphis, Tennessee, USA

The Queen of Soul, Aretha Franklin has enjoyed a long, distinguished and prolific musical career and is one of the most influential female artists of the 20th century. Renowned for her soul and R&B music, she is one of music's most versatile vocalists and has also released jazz, gospel, rock and pop numbers.

Aretha Franklin was born into a Baptist family and her father, the Reverend C.L. Franklin, encouraged his daughter's musical gifts. Aretha showed early promise as a dedicated pianist, with a powerful singing voice and her father allowed her to record her first album at the tender age of 14. Throughout her career, Franklin's music has shown a strong gospel influence, but by the time she signed with Colombia Records in 1960, her early hits were rooted more in jazz.

Although she enjoyed modest success in the early 1960s, it was not until she moved to Atlantic Records in 1967 that Franklin really hit her creative stride and was able to create her own distinctive sound. The 1967 blues ballad *I Never Loved a Man (The Way I Love You)* was quickly followed by Otis Redding's R&B number, *Respect*, the song that became Aretha's signature tune: it dominated the No. 1 spot for eight weeks and earned two Grammys in 1968.

Franklin went on to record music from several genres, as well as material she had co-written with her first husband and manager, Ted White, such as *Dr Feelgood* and *Since You've Been Gone (Sweet, Sweet Baby)*. With further hits, such as *I Say a Little Prayer* (1968), *Call Me* and *Spanish Harlem* (1971), Franklin had established herself as 'Soul Sister Number 1' by the beginning of the 1970s. She had also notched up more million-selling records than any other woman in recording history.

Franklin continued recording at a prodigious rate during the 1970s, as well as performing live at show-stopping concerts, where she became known for her flamboyant costumes and occasionally erratic behavior. When her career seemed to be flagging, her role in *The Blues Brothers* movie (1980) and the release of her album *Who's Zoomin' Who* (1985) put Aretha back in the public eye and gave her a number of pop crossover hits. She worked with the best producers in the business – Quincy Jones, Luther Vandross and Curtis Mayfield – and during the 1980s recorded with artists as varied as the Eurythmics, Dizzy Gillespie and Carlos Santana. She had another big hit with her No. 1 duet with George Michael, *I Knew You Were Waiting for Me*, in 1987.

Showered with honors, musical, political, and charitable (including 18 Grammys), Aretha Franklin has performed at two presidential inaugurations, proof, if it were needed, of her position as a highly respected and admired American musical diva.

Left: Aretha gives a characteristically spirited performance at the inauguration of President Obama in January 2009.

Right: Franklin photographed backstage in 1979, a period when her career hit a low point, before reviving in the 1980s after her performance as Mrs Matt in the movie *The Blues Brothers*.

Clark Gable

Suave, sophisticated, dashing and with a thrilling whiff of danger, Clark Gable was one of the great box-office draws of 1930s and 1940s cinema. With his classic good looks and slightly world-weary air, he epitomized masculine glamour in the glory days of Hollywood and became one of cinema's first sex symbols.

Gable appeared as an extra in silent movies during the 1920s, but turned to the stage in 1927, at the urging of his friend, the actor and director, Lionel Barrymore. Offered a contract with MGM in 1930, he was rejected by Daryl F. Zanuck of Warner Brothers, because 'His ears are too big and he looks like an ape'. Nevertheless, Gable appeared in a succession of movies for MGM, graduating from supporting roles to romantic lead and played opposite some of Hollywood's legendary leading ladies, including Norma Shearer, Greta Garbo and Joan Crawford. Gable became immensely popular with the movie-going public, who never tired of his characteristic role as a charming rough diamond.

Frank Capra's *It Happened One Night* made Gable a true star and earned him an Oscar for Best Actor in 1934. He set female pulses racing as he removed his shirt to reveal a bare chest and apparently, caused a national downturn in sales of men's undershirts. Gable bared his manly torso again for his Oscar-nominated role as Fletcher Christian in *Mutiny on the Bounty* (1935) and went on to star in a series of popular romantic comedies, earning the nickname the 'King of Hollywood' in 1938.

However, the lasting image of Clark Gable is surely from *Gone with the Wind*, the epic 1939 movie that won ten Oscars and was Hollywood's first great blockbuster. Urged by his wife, Carole Lombard, to take the role of the raffish Rhett Butler, Gable gave one of his best performances, uttering the most memorable farewell in movie history, with his 'Frankly, my dear, I don't give a damn' to Vivien Leigh's Scarlett O'Hara.

After the death of Lombard, in 1942, in a plane crash, a grief-stricken Gable joined the Army Air Corps, serving for a short while with distinction, before returning to Hollywood. He never achieved quite the same level of fame after the war and several movies were panned by the critics. But his final role, in Arthur Miller's *The Misfits* (1961), in which he starred alongside Marilyn Monroe, recaptured some of the old magic: critics, as well as Gable himself, believed it was one of his best performances.

After Gable had performed all his own stunts in his last film, his already weak heart gave out and he suffered a heart attack, just two days after shooting ended. He died ten days later, leaving his fifth wife pregnant with the son he had always longed for.

Born William Clark Gable
February 1, 1901
Cadiz, Ohio, USA

Died November 16, 1960
Los Angeles, California, USA

Left: Gable was the archetypal Hollywood idol during the golden years of the movie industry in the 1930s and 1940s.

Below: Gable in his most famous role, as Rhett Butler, with Vivien Leigh as Scarlett O'Hara, in *Gone with the Wind*.

Mohandas Gandhi

Born Mohandas Karamchand
Gandhi
October 2, 1869
Porbandar, Gujerat, India

Died 30 January, 1948
New Delhi, India

Mahatma Gandhi, 'the enlightened one,' was one of the most inspirational political leaders in history. He led the struggle for India's independence from Britain, during the first half of the 20th century, shunning the usual means of armed rebellion to advocate a policy of non-cooperation and non-violence. Gandhi's unusual protest methods inspired his followers in India and have since been adapted by political protesters and civil rights activists around the world.

Born in India, when the British Empire was at the height of its power, Gandhi trained as a lawyer in London and in 1893, began working for an Indian law firm in Durban, South Africa. Appalled by the inequalities in South African society, where Indian and black people were set apart from white people and treated as inferior races, Gandhi began to work to redress the problems of discrimination. He drew on many religious philosophies, as well as the work of writers such as Tolstoy and devised *satyagraha*, or passive resistance, as a means of righting wrongs. Faced with a public outcry against its repressive and brutal treatment of non-violent civilian protesters, Jan Smuts' government was eventually forced to concede to many of Gandhi's demands in 1914.

Gandhi returned to India in 1915 and was naturally drawn to the Indian National Congress, the political party that led the movement for Indian independence from British rule. He became the spiritual leader of the party and his policy of non-cooperation with the British included strikes and refusing to pay taxes and to respect colonial law. This was famously typified by his 240-mile 'March to the Sea' in 1930, in protest at the British salt tax. He was imprisoned several times by the British, as were thousands of his supporters, who boycotted British goods and institutions throughout India. His was not an easy path, but the action of a principled man, who profoundly believed that truth would transform society.

With the outbreak of World War II, Gandhi called for the British to 'Quit India', intensifying the revolt against British rule. The British reacted forcefully, imprisoning him for two years, but they were obliged to respect his role as spiritual figurehead of India and released him in 1944. By 1945, it was clear that power would be transferred to the Indian nation. With Partition in 1947, the states of India and Pakistan were born.

Gandhi was assassinated by a Hindu extremist on January 30, 1948, just as he had launched his fast-to-death, in an attempt to end the communal violence that had broken out across the country between the Muslim and Hindu communities. A man of great moral courage, Gandhi is revered in India as the father of the nation and upheld, globally, as a model of what can be achieved by peaceful protest.

Left: Gandhi with the leaders of the All India Conference Committee in 1942, when they decided on their campaign of civil disobedience against British rule.

Right: Imprisonment only strengthened Gandhi's cause. This photograph shows him greeting his followers after his release from jail in 1931.

Judy Garland

Born Frances Ethel Gumm
June 10, 1922
Grand Rapids, Minnesota,
USA

Died June 22, 1969
London, England

Judy Garland, one of the great stars from the age of Hollywood musicals, spent her life chasing her own rainbows, after starring as Dorothy in the Hollywood blockbuster *The Wizard of Oz* in 1939. She was admired for her versatility as an actress and singer, but her professional triumphs were overshadowed by a messy and often unhappy private life.

Blessed with a powerful voice and the kind of perky star quality so popular in 1930s and 1940s cinema, Garland first appeared on stage at the age of three. The Gumm Sisters – Judy (then Frances, or 'Baby' as she was known) and her older sisters, Suzy and Jimmie, performed on the vaudeville circuit during the 1920s and early 1930s, before changing their name to the Garland Sisters. In 1935, Judy was signed by MGM and thrust into the studio system, where looks counted for everything. Short and self-conscious, she suffered years of insecurity about her appearance. Louis B. Mayer, a man not known for his tact, called her his 'little hunchback.'

She appeared in many juvenile roles, notably with Mickey Rooney, with whom she made nine successful films, such as *Babes in Arms* (1939). The pace of filming was relentless and the studio kept its young stars focused by plying them with amphetamines and barbiturates; Garland became addicted to them. Always keen to exploit a successful formula, MGM studio perhaps prolonged her youthful roles a little too long – aged 17, Garland was playing a 12-year-old in her most famous role as Dorothy in *The Wizard of Oz* and her costume incorporated a special corset to flatten her chest. Singing the song

that is forever associated with her, *Over the Rainbow*, she won a special juvenile Oscar for the role and became one of the brightest stars in the MGM firmament.

By the mid-1940s, Garland was finally being given adult roles. She appeared in a number of celebrated musicals such as *Meet Me in St. Louis* (1944) and *The Pirate* (1948), both directed by Vincente Minnelli, her second husband (and father of her eldest daughter, Liza Minnelli). Her outstanding success in *Easter Parade* (1948) was not immediately repeated and she was unable to complete several films, because of her dependence on prescription drugs. Her third husband, Sid Luft, arranged a concert tour of Britain in 1951 and Garland played to full houses, returning to Hollywood in 1954 to give an outstanding, Oscar-nominated performance in *A Star is Born*. Garland was a legendary concert

performer and is remembered, as much for the critically acclaimed TV and concert performances she gave toward the end of her life, as for her movies. She died aged only 47, the pressure of the studio system, her personal insecurities and drug use having simply exhausted her.

Left: Garland in her most famous role, as Dorothy (with Toto the dog) in *The Wizard of Oz*.

Below: In her later career Garland was a formidable and very popular concert performer.

Bill Gates

Born William Henry Gates III
October 28, 1955
Seattle, Washington
State, USA

The brilliant founder of Microsoft is an unlikely icon, but Gates' invention of the MS-DOS computer operating system and subsequent computer software refined the personal computer and irrevocably changed the world we live in. It is perhaps truer to say that Microsoft and Windows, rather than Gates himself, are the real icons of the early 21st century.

An extremely bright child, fond of tinkering with early computers, Gates dropped out of Harvard after two years to pursue his passion for electronics and computer programming. He was more than just a technical buff – he foresaw that computers could be made to improve human lives, make businesses more efficient, operate machinery and relieve people of many humdrum chores.

He founded Microsoft with his school friend Paul Allen, an electronics expert, in 1975, working to produce programming code for Altair computers. At the time, computer programming was driven largely by amateurs as a hobby, but Gates persisted in his belief that software programmers should be paid for their work.

In the early years of Microsoft, Gates reviewed every line of code written by his staff. He was also a hardworking entrepreneur and spent much of his time negotiating deals with computer manufacturers, who needed efficient software to drive their machines. Gates could imagine a world with a computer on every desk and it was this goal that inspired him.

In 1980, Microsoft won the contract to produce an operating system for IBM's new personal computer and Gates designed an 'interface manager', which later became known as Windows. With the sale of the first Windows systems in 1985, Gates continued to pursue his vision of improving software, to make it easier and more enjoyable for everyone to use computers. He recruited the best technicians he could find and rewarded them well for their hours of hard, exacting work. He was aggressive both in positioning the Windows product and in drawing out the best from his staff.

Gates' success is legendary and made him, for many years, the world's richest person. In 2008, he stepped aside from his day job as head of Microsoft to concentrate on his charitable interests. He has become one of the most generous philanthropists in the world, using his enormous wealth to establish, along with his wife, the Bill and Melinda Gates Foundation. This has donated money to a long list of charities, including global health initiatives, education and agricultural projects around the world. Bill Gates has said that he wants to ensure 'that anyone who can reach a library can reach the internet,' and the Foundation has made a special project of equipping public libraries in the United States with computers. Alongside his charitable work, he remains non-executive chairman of Microsoft.

Left: A young Bill Gates in 1983, on the brink of fame and fortune.

Right: Gates on the roof of Microsoft headquarters in Seattle, Washington, where there are some 30,000 employees.

Marvin Gaye

Born Marvin Pentz Gay Jr.
April 2, 1939
Washington DC, USA

Died April 1, 1984
Los Angeles, California,
USA

'The Prince of Soul', Marvin Gaye was one of Motown's greatest stars in the 1960s and 1970s, charming fans with his own brand of sensual soul music.

The son of a Pentecostal minister, Marvin spent his formative musical years with the gospel choirs of his father's church. As a teenager, he turned his back on gospel music and joined a band called the Marquees, which was promoted by the producer Harvey Fuqua and renamed the Moonglows. When Fuqua moved to Detroit to work with Berry Gordy at Motown, Gay (the 'e' was added in 1962 'because it sounded more professional') went with him, as a session drummer and vocalist.

In 1961, Gaye married Berry Gordy's sister, Anna and tied himself to Motown with more than just a paper contract. Gaye released a number of records in the early 1960s, with 1964's *How Sweet It Is (To Be Loved By You)* becoming an early signature song. With Berry Gordy keen to promote Gaye's image as a romantic lover, he performed with several female artists,

memorably Tammi Terrell. Their first album, *United* (1967), produced the classics *Ain't No Mountain High Enough* and *Your Precious Love*. At the same time, Gaye enjoyed international solo success, with one of his most enduring songs, *I Heard It Through the Grapevine* (1967).

Terrell's unexpected death from a brain tumor in 1970 plunged Gaye into depression, but he emerged in 1971 with the album *What's Going On*, which is considered one of his finest works. It was his most successful solo album. Yet Motown initially refused to release it, because – influenced by jazz and funk – it marked a new departure in Gaye's soul style. It was the first Motown album to concern itself with social issues and resonated with an American pubic torn apart by the Vietnam conflict.

Empowered by this success, on his next album, Gaye concentrated on a theme that preoccupied him for the rest of his life – sex. Overtly sensual, *Let's Get it On* (1973) was Gaye's best-selling album during his lifetime. He worked with Diana

Ross on his final duet album, *Diana & Marvin*, although, after the first recording session for it, they never actually worked in the same studio at the same time.

Meanwhile Gaye's personal life was disintegrating. Divorce and drug use affected his work at the end of the 1970s, although he bounced back with the amazingly successful *Midnight Love* in 1982, which featured the masterful *Sexual Healing*, his last hit, as its first track. Sadly, Gaye could not overcome his personal demons and he was shot dead by his father during a violent family argument, a tragic end for one of the legends of soul music.

Left: Marvin Gaye in concert, 1983.

Right: 'If you cannot find peace within yourself, you will never find it anywhere else', said Gaye, who was a troubled man. His mellow music belied his inner turmoil.

Left: Archie Leach from Bristol successfully reinvented himself as one of Hollywood's most debonair and amusing actors.

Right: One of cinema's most famous scenes from *North by Northwest*, in which the innocent Roger Thornhill (Grant) is pursued by a murderous biplane.

Cary Grant

Born Archibald Alexander
Leach
January 18, 1904
Bristol, England

Died November 29, 1986
Davenport, Iowa, USA

More than any other Hollywood actor, Cary Grant came to epitomize the suave, debonair male lead, displaying time and again an air of self-possession, charm and glamour that appealed to male and female fans alike. Painstakingly crafting an image that took over his life, he somehow remained an ageless, intelligent and humorous presence on the screen for nearly 40 years.

Grant's early life was not easy. His parents were poor and his mother was institutionalized when he was nine. The young Archie developed a love of the music hall and acquired odd jobs at local theaters, before joining the Bob Pender Comedy Troupe in 1918. At the end of their two-year American tour in 1922, Archie decided to stay in the USA. He struggled to find his feet before landing his first stage role five years later.

After modest success on Broadway, he moved to Hollywood in 1931. There, Paramount executives suggested he change his name and Cary Grant was born. He appeared as little more than eye candy in his early movies, opposite some of Paramount's female stars, such as Marlene Dietrich and Mae West – whose immortal line, 'Why don't you come up sometime and see me?', was directed at him.

It was after appearing in *Sylvia Scarlett* (1935) opposite Katharine Hepburn that Grant finally found his trademark role, as a charming, if slightly unreliable character, who could be relied on to win back the heroine. He starred in a succession of 'screwball' comedies, such as *Bringing Up Baby* (1938), *Only Angels Have Wings* (1939) and *The Philadelphia Story* (1940), bucking the trend by working outside the Hollywood studio system. Unlike many of his contemporaries, Grant was not afraid of physical comedy – he used his early training in Pender's Comedy Troupe to good effect, as he conducted perfectly timed prat-falls and slapstick.

Grant remained a prime box office draw, appearing in three of Alfred Hitchcock's great thrillers, *Notorious* (1946), *To Catch a Thief* (1955) and *North by Northwest* (1959). Although his later movies did not replicate the huge success of his earlier work, none of them actually lost money and Grant decided to retire gracefully in 1966, leaving his on-screen image untarnished. He was nominated twice for Oscars and received a special Academy Award for Lifetime Achievement in 1970.

Grant's personal life was a little more tumultuous than his professional career, with five marriages, four of them ending in divorce and rumors that he was bisexual. However, he rose above all the rumors, once saying enigmatically of his screen persona, 'I pretended to be somebody I wanted to be and finally, I became that person. Or he became me.'

Che Guevara

Born Ernesto Guevara de la Serna
June 14, 1928
Rosario, Argentina

Died October 9, 1967
La Higuera, Bolivia

Immortalized on millions of posters and T-shirts around the world, Che Guevara somehow became the revolutionary's revolutionary. He believed that the troubles of Latin America could be blamed on capitalism and colonial exploitation and that world revolution was the only sure way to put things right.

Born into a middle-class family in Argentina, Guevara developed a wide range of interests, from rugby to poetry and philosophy, before training as a doctor. In 1951 he took a year off from his studies to tour South America by motorbike. He found the entire continent afflicted by problems of extreme poverty, with wealth and land concentrated in the hands of a few landlords and foreign conglomerates. He later published an account of his travels as *The Motorcycle Diaries*.

Appalled by the poverty and economic inequality he had seen, Guevara took it upon himself to change things and believed that the problems should be tackled on a continental, rather than a national level. He qualified as a doctor in 1953, but immediately left Buenos Aires for Guatemala, where the government was carrying out extensive land reforms in favor of the peasants. It was here that he met a group of Cuban exiles, notably Fidel Castro and his brother Raúl, founders of the 26th of July Movement, who were planning to overthrow the right-wing Batista regime in Cuba. Guevara joined them, seeing in their struggle exactly the kind of just, anti-capitalist cause he was seeking.

Working initially as the combat medic, Guevara trained with the revolutionaries and adapted to military life with gusto.

He fought with distinction during the campaign from 1956 to 1959, making an impression as a well-respected leader, a skilled tactician and a harsh disciplinarian.

After the revolution, Castro appointed Guevara to the post of Cuban Finance Minister, a job that enabled him to pursue his goal of a truly socialist economy. From 1964, Che worked as an ambassador for the new Cuban regime, making a tour of eastern bloc countries to strengthen diplomatic ties and secure their investment in Cuba. Che's natural charm and commitment to the socialist cause played a crucial part in ensuring the Soviet Union's involvement in Cuba. This led directly to the Bay of Pigs confrontation with the USA in 1961 and the Cuban Missile Crisis of 1962, when the world was brought to the brink of nuclear war.

After continuing his work as a revolutionary diplomat for Cuba until 1965, Che moved on to work in the Congo and then Bolivia. There, he was finally caught by CIA-funded soldiers and executed. Reviled by the right and hailed as a hero by the left, thanks to his intelligence and charisma Guevara is still regarded as an iconic figure 40 years after his death.

Left: Engaging, charming and committed, revolutionary Che Guevara travelled the world in search of wrongs to right.

Below: A poster for the Cuban movie, *Che Today and Forever*.

DOCUMENTAL CUBANO DIRECTOR: PEDRO CHASKEL

che che che CHE HOY Y SIEMPRE che CHE CHE

Rolf Harris

Born March 30, 1930
Bassendean, Perth,
Western Australia

Painter, musician, composer and all-round entertainer, Rolf Harris has shone in an impressively wide range of fields and has come to be seen as an artist and educator in his own right.

Initially a television cartoonist, Harris went on to write and record enduring hit singles, such as *Sun Arise* (1962), which went to No. 2 in the UK charts, while also playing jazz and continuing to paint and draw. He has received many honors, including Commander of the Order of the British Empire (2006) and Member of the Order of Australia (1989), but perhaps the greatest was the commission to paint a portrait of Queen Elizabeth II for her 80th birthday in 2005.

A champion swimmer in his teens, Harris won a radio 'Amateur Hour' competition at the age of 18. After studying at the University of Western Australia, he arrived in England in 1952 to attend art school in Kennington, south London. Almost immediately he got involved in the early days of television, with a five-minute cartoon-drawing slot on the BBC.

In 1960, he returned to Perth to produce and star in a weekday children's program, as well as hosting his own weekly variety show. In the same year, he wrote and recorded his first hit single, the comic *Tie Me Kangaroo Down, Sport*, which has become his theme tune. Ever quick to recognize a trend, he wrote a special version of the song for The Beatles and performed it with them in 1963. *Sun Arise*, a more serious and lyrical aboriginal-style song, which introduced the didgeridoo (an indigenous Australian wind instrument) to western audiences, was beaten to the No. 1 spot by Elvis Presley in 1962.

In 1969, Harris had a surprise No. 1 UK hit – and his most successful single – with his re-recording of the old music hall tear-jerker *Two Little Boys*, about two friends who grow up to fight in the American Civil War. By 1973, he was sufficiently well established to perform the opening concert at the newly completed Sydney Opera House.

Television has remained his principal medium, however. He has appeared in a string of shows, initially as presenter and then in 1967, with *The Rolf Harris Show*, which remained a light entertainment staple throughout the 1970s and 1980s. He also starred in a number of television shows, such as *Rolf's Cartoon Club*, which focused more specifically on his artistic gifts. Many of his appearances were marked by him dashing off large pictures at speed and apparently effortlessly and at some point, asking the audience: 'Can you tell what it is yet?' Between 2001 and 2007, he presented *Rolf on Art*, in which he both introduced and imitated the work of notable artists. His portrait of Queen Elizabeth featured in a special edition of the program and in 2002, London's National Gallery featured an exhibition of his art.

Right: Rolf Harris has enjoyed an extraordinary 40-year career as a TV presenter, artist and musician. His appeal shows no sign of diminishing with his advancing years.

Below: Harris sketching a picture of Bambi for a TV audience in 1986.

Stephen Hawking

Born Stephen William Hawking
January 8, 1942
Oxford, England

The gifted theoretical physicist, Stephen Hawking, has achieved celebrity status by using the power of mathematics to advance our understanding of the universe.

Hawking has had a globally recognized scientific career, while his publications and public appearances have been hugely successful in explaining complex science to the general public. This is all the more astonishing, given that, since his early twenties, he has suffered from a type of motor neurone disease, which has progressively incapacitated him and talks only with the aid of a voice synthesizer.

After obtaining a first at the University of Oxford and a PhD at Cambridge, Hawking had his initial significant breakthrough, in collaboration with mathematician Roger Penrose, with their work on gravitational singularities – places in space, or time at which some quantity becomes infinite – in relation to Einstein's theory of general relativity. At the time, the most favored theory regarding the nature of the universe was the 'steady-state' theory, which saw it as having always existed. Penrose and Hawking built on Penrose's work in identifying the point inside a black hole where all mass shrinks to nothing – a 'singularity' – to argue that Einstein's concept of space/time must have an ending, in just such a final point.

Hawking then applied the argument to theories about the origins of the universe. He theorized that this had taken the form of a black hole in reverse and had begun as a singularity, an infinitesimal point containing the entire substance of the universe. This was the 'big-bang' theory, first proposed in the 1920s and now widely accepted as a result of Hawking's work. Since then, he has worked on identifying a theoretical link between general relativity, which deals with gravity and the other great scientific development of the earlier 20th century, quantum theory, which deals with miniscule events inside the atom. This is the unified field theory that Einstein unsuccessfully sought to define.

Recognition for Hawking's work was not slow in coming. In 1974, he was named a member of the prestigious UK scientific body, the Royal Society, at the unusually young age of 32. In 1979, he became Lucasian Professor of Mathematics at the University of Cambridge, a post he held for 30 years, until he retired in 2009. His book *A Brief History of Time: From the Big Bang to Black Holes* (1988) outlined his theories in terms intended to be comprehensible to non-scientists. The book spent over four years in the best-seller charts and Hawking followed it up in 2001, with *The Universe in a Nutshell*. He was made a Companion of Honour by Queen Elizabeth II in 1989 and was awarded the Presidential Medal of Freedom, the highest civilian honor in the US, in 2009.

Left: Hawking lecturing in Berlin, 2005.

Right: Stephen Hawking has overcome his considerable physical limitations to pursue a stellar career as the world's most famous theoretical physicist.

Jimi Hendrix

Born Johnny Allen Hendrix
November 27, 1942
Seattle, Washington, USA

Died September 18, 1970
London, England

Brilliant and original, the legendary rock musician, Jimi Hendrix, is often hailed as the greatest electric guitarist in the history of rock music. In his short life he established a riotous reputation, with his outrageous fashion sense and breathtakingly uncontrolled stage performances.

A self-taught guitarist, Hendrix initially worked as a backing musician, after two years in the US Army. By the time he moved to New York in 1964, he had played with some of the big names of the time, notably Sam Cooke, Little Richard and Wilson Pickett. In New York, he formed his first band, the Blue Flame. He moved to London in 1966, after meeting ex-Animals bassist Chas Chandler, who signed him as a performer and helped him to form a new band – the Jimi Hendrix Experience – with Noel Redding and Mitch Mitchell. Their first three singles, *Hey Joe*, *Stone Free* and *Purple Haze*, were all hits and their first album *Are You Experienced* (1967) became a blueprint for the potential of the electric guitar, which was recorded on four tracks and then mixed into mono. It made Hendrix a superstar and paved the way for other psychedelic and experimental rock acts.

Hendrix's stage performance began to develop at the same time. Booked as one of the opening acts on the Walker Brothers' farewell tour in March 1967, he set his guitar on fire at the end of his set and was warned by Rank Theatre management to tone down his suggestive stage act. The burning and smashing of a guitar became an integral part of the Hendrix act and a similar performance, at the Monterey International Pop Festival in California, was caught on film in 1968.

The next two albums, *Axis: Bold as Love* and the even more experimental *Electric Ladyland* made 1968 the band's most commercially successful year. But this was a high point. Hendrix came under pressure from Black Power supporters to form an all-black band, Chandler became frustrated with Hendrix's perfectionism and left and the Jimi Hendrix Experience finally broke up in 1969.

Hendrix's appearance with a scratch band at the Woodstock Festival in 1969 was a memorable one; it ended with his solo improvisation of *The Star-Spangled Banner*, now regarded as an iconic event of the era. In August 1970, with new manager Michael Jeffery, Hendrix opened his own recording studio, the Electric Lady Studios, in Greenwich Village, New York, which was designed especially for him; the aim was to offer a professional, yet relaxing recording environment to stimulate his creativity.

A European tour came first, however and a restless Hendrix cut some of his gigs short, earning booing and jeering at his final concert performance. Two weeks later, tragically young, he was dead, apparently from a drugs overdose, but in circumstances which remain mysterious.

Left: Hendrix pictured at the Monterey Pop Festival 1967, the day of his debut performance in North America.

Below: Hendrix gives a virtuoso performance in Boston in June 1970, shortly before his death.

Audrey Hepburn

Elegant, gamine and classically beautiful, Audrey Hepburn was a Hollywood goddess.

The star of over 25 movies, she became an actress almost by accident, but won an Oscar for her first Hollywood movie in 1954 and was nominated four more times over the course of her career.

Born in Belgium in 1929 and with Dutch, German and Bohemian relatives, Hepburn spoke five languages and spent her childhood shuttling between Europe and Britain. She trained first as a ballerina, but progressed to cabaret and revues and in 1951, to the movies in Britain. Cast as the eponymous *Gigi* in 1951, Hepburn's appearance on Broadway quite literally put her name in lights, where they remained for the rest of her career.

From Broadway, it was just a plane ride to Hollywood and in 1953, her first Hollywood movie, the charming and witty *Roman Holiday*, cast her opposite Gregory Peck and won her the Best Actress Oscar in 1954. Her signature style – restrained elegance, slightly unworldly, with a hint of promise – carried her through several films with some of Hollywood's finest actors and directors, such as Billy Wilder, John Huston, Humphrey Bogart and Cary Grant. A tall, slim woman, her natural grace and dancer's carriage were enhanced by the clothes of Givenchy, who dressed her for her next film, *Sabrina* (1954) and continued to design for her for the next

35 years. By the end of the 1950s, Hepburn was not only one of Hollywood's hottest stars but also, partly thanks to Givenchy, one of the most stylish women in the world.

She is probably best remembered, though, for her role as Holly Golightly in *Breakfast at Tiffany's* (1961), the film that came to epitomize her elfin grace, charm and sophistication. Naturally shy, Hepburn found it a challenge to portray such an extrovert character, but the role earned her another Oscar nomination. During the 1960s, she went on to star as Eliza Doolittle with Rex Harrison in *My Fair Lady* (with the vocals famously voiced by Marni Nixon), with Peter O'Toole in *How to Steal a Million* and with Albert Finney in *Two for the Road.*

Hepburn spent most of the 1970s, in semi-retirement, bringing up her two sons and working as a goodwill ambassador for UNICEF. Her wartime experiences, when she lived in the Netherlands under Nazi occupation, remained with her and she devoted a great deal of time to improving the lives of disadvantaged children around the world.

Her status as one of the world's most beautiful and elegant women seemed to mystify her, as she much preferred casual clothes and never felt that she was especially beautiful. Like it or not, the still of her in large hat with an oversized cigarette holder from *Breakfast at Tiffany's* remains a classic movie image and her 'little black dress' (by Givenchy) from the same film sold at auction in December 2006 for nearly one million dollars.

Born	Audrey Kathleen Ruston May 4, 1929 Ixelles, Belgium
Died	January 20, 1993 Tolochenaz, Switzerland

Right: Audrey Hepburn on the set of *Breakfast at Tiffany's.*

Left: Audrey Hepburn at the Studio de Boulogne, during the making of *How to Steal a Million* in Paris.

Above: Soon after becoming a UNICEF ambassador, Audrey Hepburn went on a mission to Ethiopia, where years of drought and civil strife had caused terrible famine.

Sir Edmund Hillary

Born Edmund Percival Hillary
July 20, 1919
Auckland, New Zealand

Died January 11, 2008
Auckland, New Zealand

In May 1953, mountaineer and explorer Edmund Hillary, together with Sherpa Tenzing Norgay, became the first man to reach the summit of Mount Everest in the Himalayas, the highest mountain in the world.

A New Zealander by birth, Hillary first became interested in climbing during a school trip and made his first major climb in 1939, in the southern Alps. After studying at the University of Auckland, he took up beekeeping in the summer, in order to leave the winter months free for mountaineering.

During the 1940s, he made many climbs in New Zealand and then in Europe, establishing a reputation for daring, strength and reliability. He joined a reconnaissance expedition to Everest in 1951; the route from Tibet was blocked by China and the Nepalese permitted only one attempt a year on the alternative, southern, route. In 1952, Hillary was one of those invited by the Joint Himalayan Committee to join the planned official British expedition, under Sir John Hunt, in 1953.

A joint effort, comprising 400 people, the expedition set up its base camp – still today the starting point for Everest attempts – in March. By late May, it had worked its way up to the final camp, at 8,000 m (25,900 ft). Two climbers attempted the summit first, but had to turn back when an oxygen system failed and Hunt named Hillary and Tenzing as the next team to try. On May 29, they succeeded in reaching the summit – at 8,500 m (29,000 ft) one of the last untrodden places on earth. News of their success reached the UK on the day of Queen Elizabeth II's coronation and the group was stunned by the international reaction: Hillary was knighted only a week later, on June 6.

Further expeditions to the Himalayas followed in the 1950s and 1960s and Hillary also joined the Commonwealth Trans-Antarctic Expedition in 1958, leading the New Zealand section. His group was the first to reach the South Pole overland since Amundsen in 1911 and Scott in 1912. In 1974, he led an expedition by jet boat up the River Ganges to its source and in 1985, he accompanied astronaut Neil Armstrong on a flight that landed at the North Pole. In so doing, he became the first man to have stood at both poles and on top of the world.

After his Everest success, Hillary founded the Himalayan Trust, with the aim of helping the Sherpa people of Nepal and oversaw the building of schools and hospitals there. He was also honorary president of the American Himalayan Foundation, which focuses on the ecology of the region and of Mountain Wilderness, a worldwide body dedicated to mountain protection.

Left: A smiling Hillary with Sherpa Tenzing at base camp after their descent from Everest in June 1953.

Below: Hillary went on to explore the Antarctic with the Vivian Fuchs expedition in 1958.

Michael Jackson

Born Michael Joseph Jackson
August 29, 1958
Gary, Indiana, USA

Died June 25, 2009
Los Angeles, California,
USA

Known as the King of Pop, Michael Jackson was quite simply the most successful entertainer of all time.

Jackson was the world's biggest-selling solo artist, with sales in excess of 750 million albums. His undeniable vocal talent was complemented by a distinctive musical style, superbly choreographed dance moves and a private life that can best be described as idiosyncratic. The combination of his gentle and childlike public persona, enormous personal wealth and all-conquering musical talent made him one of the great musical icons of the late 20th and early 21st centuries.

The eighth child of ten, Jackson made his first stage appearance in 1964, alongside his elder brothers and two years later, became a permanent member of the Jackson 5. Aggressively promoted by their father, Joe, the band were signed by the Motown label in 1969. During the early 1970s, their energetic and appealing performances made them one of pop's biggest acts. Crowds of screaming girls – as many white as black – accompanied every public appearance. Young Michael stood out from his brothers, partly because of his age and size, but more importantly, because of his enormous talent.

The release of the solo album *Off the Wall,* in 1979, signaled the beginning of a phenomenal solo career. When *Thriller* was released in 1982, rumors of Jackson's personal strangeness merely fueled the fans' ardor. Critics and peers, however, united in their praise of his vocal skills and mastery of the pop genre.

Thriller was marked by the release of what has become one of the most famous music videos ever. It was one of the first to combine a complex storyline, fabulous and much-copied choreography and amazing special effects to produce an innovative and highly influential film. The man who gave the world unique dance moves, such as the moonwalk, continued to dazzle audiences throughout the 1980s and the album *Bad*, released in 1986, generated five No. 1 singles.

By the early 1990s, Jackson's private life had begun to dominate the headlines. Allegations of plastic surgery, skin lightening and close relationships with young boys at Neverland – his ranch retreat-cum-personal theme park in California – clouded his reputation and attracted widespread ridicule. His two short-lived marriages (firstly to Lisa Marie Presley, the only daughter of Elvis Presley and secondly to Debbie Rowe, a nurse) were regarded as shams. Allegations of child abuse, in 1994 and again in 2005, threatened to overwhelm both his personal and professional standing and he was driven to near bankruptcy.

Nevertheless, Jackson's sudden and premature death, in June 2009, was a huge shock to millions of fans around the world, who had remained loyal to him throughout the tribulations and provoked an outpouring of grief for an unassailable talent. The bizarre rumors that had surrounded his lifestyle contributed to his status as a musical icon almost as much as the music itself.

Left: Michael Jackson dancing during his performance in Munich's Olympic stadium on June 27, 1999.

Below: A young Michael Jackson talking on the phone in April 1971.

Sir Peter Jackson

Born Peter Robert Jackson
October 31, 1961
Pukerua Bay, New
Zealand

Peter Jackson seemed an improbable director to film J.R.R. Tolkien's epic fantasy series *The Lord of the Rings*. But in the event, his vision and commitment proved inspired and the result was a barn-storming Oscar-laden success.

Born in New Zealand, Jackson became a fan of film-maker Ray Harryhausen's mix of animation and live action and of the television series *Thunderbirds*.
He began making short films, learning on the job and his first feature, the 1987 horror comedy *Bad Taste* – a team effort with friends, shot largely at weekends – gained a cult following. When two more gore-infested movies followed – *Meet the Feebles* (1989), shot with Muppet-style puppets, and the zombie horror *Braindead* (1992) – Jackson's style seemed established.

The lurid black comedy *Heavenly Creatures* (1994), however, proved otherwise. Based on real events, it is a chilling tale of two teenage girls, who concoct a shared fantasy world that turns murderous. The movie launched Kate Winslet's career, gained Jackson an Oscar nomination for Best Screenplay and led to his first big budget Hollywood film, *The Frighteners* (1996), starring Michael J. Fox.

By then, Jackson had already begun negotiations for the film rights to the supposedly unfilmable *The Lord of the Rings*, with the aim of making a serious fantasy film, which would exploit the new developments in computer-generated imagery (CGI). The deal-making proved tortuous, with the trilogy reduced first to two films and then to one. Finally, in 1998, a new backer gave Jackson the go-ahead to shoot all three films back-to-back in his native New Zealand.

The project involved planning on an epic scale: 150 different locations were used; the New Zealand army helped to build Hobbiton months before shooting, so that the planting would be mature; and a premier cast spent over a year on location, forming a strong bond in the process. Marketing began 18 months before the release of the first film, *The Fellowship of the Ring*, in December 2001; the online promotional trailer registered 1.7 million download hits in its first 24 hours. The film's pulsing soundtrack and gritty realism, together with its epic theme of good versus evil, chimed with a public facing overseas war and domestic terrorism and won four Oscars. Its two successors were released in the following two years, with the final installment, *The Return of the King* (2003), winning all the 11 Oscars for which it was nominated, an extraordinary achievement.

Jackson has followed this up with a successful version of *King Kong* (2005), for which Universal paid him a record upfront salary of $20 million. An adaptation of the best-selling novel *The Lovely Bones* (2009) was less well received. Undaunted, he is now working on a two-part adaptation of Tolkien's first novel, *The Hobbit*. In 2010, he was knighted by Queen Elizabeth II.

Right: Peter Jackson brandishes one of the 11 Oscars won in 2004 for *The Return of the King*.

Below: Jackson was apparently inspired to become a film director when he watched the 1933 version of *King Kong* as a child. He released his version in 2005, pocketing the highest advance ever paid to a film director.

Sir Elton John

Born Reginald Kenneth Dwight
March 25, 1947
Pinner, Middlesex,
England

A flamboyant and durable singer, songwriter and pianist, Elton John has sold more than 250 million records in his 40-year career.

Young Reginald Dwight (he formally took the name Elton Hercules John in 1972) was a talented pianist from an early age. He won a junior scholarship to London's Royal Academy of Music at the age of 11 and began his musical career as a pub pianist. His first band, Bluesology, toured with some big names, including Long John Baldry and in 1967, he began a song-writing partnership with lyricist

Bernie Taupin that still continues today. He launched his solo singing career with the album *Empty Sky* (1969); a follow-up, *Elton John* (1970), was his first solo hit and established his music as a successful blend of pop and rock. A stream of well-received albums followed and by 1972, he had formed the Elton John Band, which performed both as instrumental players and as strong backing vocalists.

Much of John's commercial success in the 1970s was due to his impassioned performances, extravagant piano style and famous stage image, complete with outrageous costumes and monster glasses. Perhaps the hottest act in the rock world, he filled venues worldwide. Seven albums in a row reached the UK No. 1 slot, between 1972 and 1975 and produced a string of hit singles, like *Rocket Man,* while his memorable duet with Kiki Dee, *Don't Go Breaking My Heart,* topped both US and the UK charts in 1976.

A period in the doldrums followed, with the occasional hit and much personal upheaval.

This included a brief marriage to an old friend in 1984, which ended four years later when John finally confirmed that he was gay. At about the same time, he underwent throat surgery, which resulted in the loss of his famous falsetto voice.

A No. 1 hit in 1990 with *Sacrifice* saw the start of a happier and more productive period. The songs John wrote jointly with Tim Rice for the Disney film *The Lion King* (1994) gained three Oscar nominations, with the Best Song award going to *Can You Feel the Love Tonight*. John also founded the Elton John AIDS Foundation in 1992 and has dedicated a proportion of his earnings to AIDS-related research ever since. Personal happiness arrived in 1993, when he met David Furnish, now his civil partner. In September 1997, John performed a special version of his single *Candle in the Wind* to emotive effect at the funeral of Diana, Princess of Wales. The recorded version has sold over 37 million copies and a knighthood followed in 1998.

Elton John's song-writing success peaked with the music for the runaway West End and Broadway success, *Billy Elliot the Musical* (2005). John continues to tour to huge acclaim, celebrating his 60th birthday in 2007 with a record-breaking 60th concert at Madison Square Garden, New York.

Left: Elton and his writing partner Bernie Taupin, 1971. Taupin has penned the lyrics for most of Elton's hits.

Far left: Elton began his career as a pub pianist at the age of 15. Half a century later, his presence fills arenas all over the world.

Michael Jordan

Born Michael Jeffrey Jordan
February 17, 1963
Brooklyn, New York, USA

Professional basketball player, phenomenal athlete and shrewd businessman, Michael Jordan is generally regarded as the greatest basketball player of all time. He raised the National Basketball Association to worldwide superstardom in the 1980s and 1990s.

Born in Brooklyn, Jordan moved as a child to North Carolina with his family. At high school, he tried out for the basketball team, but at 5 ft 11 in (1.8 m) he was told he was too short. However, the next year he grew 4 in (10 cm) and made the team, earning a basketball scholarship in 1981 to the University of North Carolina at Chapel Hill. In both 1983 and 1984, he was selected for the NCAA All-American First Team. He won a gold medal in the 1984 Olympics in Los Angeles and left college a year early to join the Chicago Bulls.

Jordan won Rookie of the Year Award in his first season with the Bulls and immediately established himself with fans everywhere. In his first game at Madison Square Garden in New York, against the New York Knicks, he received a standing ovation. Attendances, both at home in the Chicago Stadium and on the road, rose dramatically and just a month into his professional career, Jordan was featured on the cover of *Sports Illustrated* under the headline 'A Star is Born.' He played a versatile game and was known for his power and agility on court, his leadership abilities, his prolific scoring and his extraordinary leaps to the basket, which earned him the nicknames 'Air Jordan' and 'His Airness.' Sponsorship offers followed and Jordan became known for his astute product endorsements – Air Jordan Nike trainers still remain popular today.

From the 1987–8 season onward, Jordan notched up a long sequence of record-breaking achievements. He was the first player since Wilt Chamberlin to score 3,000 points in a single season. In 1988, he received the NBA Most Valuable Player Award, a feat repeated in 1991, 1992, 1996 and 1998. The Bulls won their first NBA championship in 1991 and won it again in 1992 and 1993, securing a 'three-peat.'

Though traumatized by the murder of his father in July 1993, when he retired temporarily from the game, Jordan returned strongly in 1995 to help the Bulls win the championship again. He also starred in the mixed live action/animation film *Space Jam* (1996). In the following season, he started all 82 games – the Bulls won 72 of them and took the championship yet again – and averaged 30.4 points.

Jordan retired again in 1999, becoming part-owner of the Washington Wizards. He returned to play for a couple of seasons, but retired for good in 2003. In 2009, he was named greatest North American athlete of the 20th century by US cable TV network ESPN and was inducted into the Basketball Hall of Fame.

Left and right: Michael Jordan enjoyed a stunning career as the most famous and successful basketball player in the world, gaining lucrative sponsorships from some of the world's major brands.

Grace Kelly

Born Grace Patricia Kelly
November 12, 1929
Philadelphia,
Pennsylvania, USA

Died September 14, 1982
Monaco

An exquisitely beautiful actress, who brought genuine glamour and style to her film-making, Grace Kelly, passed briefly, but memorably, through Hollywood to become a real-life princess.

Her father, the son of Irish immigrants, was an athlete and self-made millionaire and Kelly was brought up in high Philadelphia style. She attended the prestigious American Academy of Dramatic Arts in New York, where her graduation performance was in *The Philadelphia Story*. Her first acting roles were on stage and she made her Broadway debut in Strindberg's *The Father*, alongside Raymond Massey. She was Gary Cooper's choice for her first starring role, as his demure Quaker bride in *High Noon* (1952). As with many of her later films, rumors were rife of an on-set affair between Kelly and her leading man.

Meanwhile, Kelly had landed a seven-year contract with MGM, her first film being the supporting role in *Mogambo* (1953), with Clark Gable and Ava Gardner, for which she won an Oscar nomination. Oddly, her one Oscar-winning role was a non-glamorous one in *The Country Girl* (1954), where she played the long-suffering wife of alcoholic has-been actor, Bing Crosby. In 1956, she played the haughty rich girl in the delightful MGM musical *High Society* (1956), an update of *The Philadelphia Story*.

But it was the pairing with director Alfred Hitchcock that made Kelly truly memorable. One of a series of signature blonde actresses with whom Hitchcock did some of his best work, Kelly played the beautiful, vulnerable, yet ambiguous heroine in *Dial M for Murder* (1954), the victim of husband Ray Milland's devious plotting. Next, Hitchcock cast her with James Stewart in the gripping *Rear Window* (1954). Stewart played the part of a news photographer encased in plaster, who risks both his own and his girlfriend's (Kelly) life investigating what he believes to be a murder. Kelly's final outing for Hitchcock was yet another alluring and equivocal role, flirting with and entrapping Cary Grant's retired jewel thief in the romantic comedy *To Catch a Thief* (1956). The chemistry between the stars was such that Kelly's future husband did his best to bury the finished film.

In 1955, Kelly met Prince Rainier of Monaco when she led the US delegation at the Cannes Film Festival. She married him a year later in a sumptuous ceremony in Monaco Cathedral. From then on she devoted her life to creating the role of gracious and immaculate princess consort. The occasional offers of a starring role – as the lead in Hitchcock's *Marnie* in 1962, for instance – were firmly rejected. In 1982, at the age of 52, Kelly had a stroke at the wheel of her car on a precipitous mountain road and died from the injuries sustained in the crash.

Right: With her classically beautiful features, Grace Kelly epitomized the Hollywood goddess.

Left: Kelly's longest role was as princess consort to her husband, Prince Rainier of Monaco, after their 1955 marriage, in which old world royalty merged with new world glamour.

John F. Kennedy

Born John Fitzgerald Kennedy
May 29, 1917
Brookline, Massachusetts,
USA

Died November 22, 1963
Dallas, Texas, USA

JFK – reforming Democratic politician and American statesman, 35th president of the USA and assassination victim – is one of the totemic figures of the 20th century.

Kennedy was no stranger to power. His multi-millionaire father had been a supporter of Roosevelt's New Deal to rescue the US from the Depression and served as the US ambassador in London. A brilliant student, JFK studied at both Harvard and London universities and was decorated for his wartime service as a torpedo boat commander in the Pacific. His already troublesome back was further damaged in action and though he underwent several spine operations in the 1950s, he spent much of the rest of his life in pain.

Returning to a political career, he entered the House of Representatives in 1947 and the Senate in 1952. In 1953, he married Jacqueline Lee Bouvier, who was to become as iconic in her own right as her famous husband. By 1956, he was already sufficiently well established to come second in the nominations for presidential running mate to Adlai Stevenson, who then lost the election to Eisenhower.

Declaring his intention to run for president himself in January 1960, Kennedy established himself as a candidate with broad popular appeal, despite the suspicion among conservative Protestants of his Catholicism. The series of televised debates between JFK and his republican rival, Richard 'Tricky Dicky' Nixon, which Kennedy, the more relaxed and authoritative performer, was deemed to have won, marked a milestone moment when TV was recognized as a dominant force in politics.

Defeating Nixon to become the second youngest and first Catholic president, Kennedy entered the White House on a wave of popular enthusiasm and his 1,000-day tenure came to be dubbed 'the Camelot years.' His inspiring inaugural address ('Ask not what your country can do for you; ask what you can do for your country') struck a note of international idealism that chimed well with the new decade.

Even so, the election was one of the closest in history and JFK's liberal domestic 'new frontier' policies, involving tax and social reforms and further racial integration, were significantly shackled by a conservative Congress. The abortive Bay of Pigs invasion of Cuba in 1961, planned by his predecessor to depose Castro, was undoubtedly a factor in Castro's agreement to a Soviet missile site in Cuba. This, in turn, precipitated the Cuban Missile Crisis of October 1962, which brought the world to the brink of nuclear confrontation.

Having established cordial relations with USSR premier Khrushchev, however, JFK achieved a nuclear test-ban treaty with him and the UK in 1963. His murder in Dallas in November 1963, ostensibly by a lone assassin, Lee Harvey Oswald, remains the subject of debate and many conspiracy theories.

Left: Kennedy was an impassioned public speaker, who inspired audiences.

Right: The Kennedys in the motorcade in Dallas minutes before the president's assassination, November 22, 1963.

Martin Luther King Jr.

Born January 15, 1929
Atlanta, Georgia, USA

Died April 4, 1968
Memphis, Tennessee, USA

Martin Luther King's fiery oratory inspired both black people and white people to believe that the world could be a better place, where people of all beliefs and colors could live together peacefully and equally.

The son of a Baptist pastor, Martin Luther King followed his father into the church and assumed his first ministry in 1955, in Montgomery, Alabama, in the heart of the segregated southern states of the USA. He immediately worked with the leaders of the Montgomery bus boycott, when black people boycotted the local buses for over a year to protest against segregation. Eventually the bus company was driven to near bankruptcy and the US Supreme Court was forced to declare segregation on the Montgomery buses illegal.

King went on to found the Southern Leadership Christian Conference (SCLC) in 1957, to protest further against discrimination and advance the civil rights cause. Unlike many of his radical colleagues, King admired the ideals of Gandhi and advocated nonviolent protest to force the government to accept African-American demands for equality. He believed that media coverage of well-organized protests against the South's discriminatory laws would politicize Americans and push the civil rights issue to the top of the political agenda.

King's oratory, organization and righteous moral anger galvanized public opinion. Mass protests against discrimination in Birmingham, Alabama, throughout 1963 led to thousands of arrests and violent clashes between protesters and police, as well as between the white population and civil rights activists. Attacked many times himself, King was arrested and jailed for his part in the protest. Undeterred, he led the largest of the civil rights protests, the March on Washington in August 1963, when he faced a crowd of 250,000 and inspired listeners around the world with his 'I have a dream' speech. He articulated a simple vision of freedom and justice for all and his actions led directly to the landmark 1964 Civil Rights Act, which outlawed racial segregation. The Nobel Peace Prize in 1964 signaled international recognition for King's work.

The protests continued, culminating in the violent Selma to Montgomery marches in 1965, when King led the campaign for black voter registration. His message of peaceful protest had proven effective, but the pace of change was too slow for many and the civil rights movement lost its unity. King's dream ended abruptly when he was shot in Memphis, Tennessee, in 1968 and the riots that shook several American cities in the aftermath of his death were a tribute to the esteem in which he was held. Black America felt it had lost its protector.

However, King's work for the civil rights movement of America was a lasting legacy. He is still revered as a formidable human rights activist and a courageous man who overcame enormous prejudice to better the lot of humanity.

Right and below: Throughout his career, Martin Luther King was renowned for his oratory, which managed to be both inspirational and measured. He urged black people to stand up and protest peacefully for their civil rights, while warning against violent action.

Led Zeppelin

Formed 1968
Disbanded 1980

Members John Bonham 1948–80
John Paul Jones 1946–present
Jimmy Page 1944–present
Robert Plant 1948–present

Led Zeppelin were the most successful British rock band of the 1970s.

The band emerged in the dying days of the 1960s, from the demise of the Yardbirds. Guitarist Jimmy Page recruited John Paul Jones, drummer John Bonham and vocalist Robert Plant to his band, the New Yardbirds, in 1968. They recorded their first album in a record 30 hours and changed the band's name to Led Zeppelin, at the suggestion of The Who's Keith Moon.

Embarking on a tour of the US, they were delighted when their first album, *Led Zeppelin* (1969), reached the Billboard Top 10 within just two months. Led Zeppelin's sound was like no other at the time, with carefully arranged screaming guitar riffs, distorted amplification and amazingly loud vocals. It was the beginning of heavy metal. But the band were not just guitar thrashers – they also had a sensitive side, displayed to great effect in their most famous song, *Stairway to Heaven* (1971), which builds slowly from almost madrigal-like melodies to a full-blown hard rock-fest. Both Page and Plant were heavily influenced by blues music and both had an interest in the occult and mythology, which showed itself in mystical (and occasionally mystifying) lyrics.

The release of *Led Zeppelin II* was an even greater success than their debut album, reaching the No. 1 chart position in both the UK and US. It was recorded in a year packed with concert tours – four in the US and four in Britain. The album's first track, *Whole Lotta Love*, was a massive hit in the US, but the band generally resisted issuing singles, believing that each album was an entire musical entity and a listening experience in itself.

In 1973, the band's tour of the US broke box office records set by The Beatles and two years later, with concert and record sales from their albums at a new high, they were officially the most popular rock band in the world. In the mid-1970s, Led Zeppelin came to epitomize rock star excess, traveling by a private jet nicknamed 'The Starship' and trashing hotels.

After the formation of their record label Swan Song, the band released their first double album, *Physical Graffiti*, in 1975, which became their biggest selling record and a critical success. With *Presence* (1976), Led Zeppelin abandoned their mild flirtation with Celtic and folk influences to return to heavy rock and *In Through the Out Door* was the group's last album, recorded in 1978. Their next tour in 1980 was abandoned, when John Bonham died and the group reluctantly decided to split. Page and Plant have since had successful solo careers, but nothing has recaptured the sheer flamboyance and hard rocking glory of Led Zeppelin at the peak of their career.

Above: Robert Plant, John Bonham and Jimmy Page in 1970, after receiving the *Melody Maker* pop poll award for the best British group.

Right: Plant on stage in New York, 1988.

Bruce Lee

Born Lee Jun Fan
November 27, 1940
San Francisco, California,
USA

Died July 20, 1973
Hong Kong

Bruce Lee almost single-handedly revived the West's interest in martial arts during the 1960s and 1970s, with a string of Hong Kong-and Hollywood-produced action movies. A diminutive dynamo, Lee moved with lightning speed, flying through the air to land punches and kicks precisely where they were needed.

Lee was born in San Francisco, but grew up in Hong Kong. Life was not entirely easy for the young Lee on the gang-filled streets of postwar Hong Kong: though his family was wealthy, Lee was constantly involved in street fights. This inspired him to take up martial arts and from the age of 13, he trained under the great master, Yip Man. In 1959, his parents sent him back to the US to university, where he studied drama at the University of Washington. He also began to teach martial arts and in 1964, he dropped out of college to teach full time.

Lee developed his own approach, abandoning the rigid and formal drills of traditional systems in favor of flexibility, speed and efficiency, as well as encouraging weight training and running to build strength and stamina. He called his system Jeet Kune Do, or 'the Way of the Intercepting Fist.' Working with leading US martial arts enthusiasts, such as the karate expert Ed Parker and the taekwondo master Jhoon Rhee, Lee made guest appearances at popular martial arts events, notably the Long Beach International Karate Championships and opened two martial arts schools.

As his profile rose, Lee was invited to audition for the TV series *The Green Hornet,* in which he appeared as Kato, the sidekick and bodyguard. He received more fan mail than the show's star and his performance inspired thousands to take up martial arts. Lee capitalized on this success, by providing personalized martial arts training for stars, such as Steve McQueen and James Coburn and his invaluable Hollywood connections led to guest appearances in a couple of films. He quickly became disillusioned, however, as it became clear that Hollywood was unlikely to cast him in a leading role and he returned to Hong Kong in 1971.

Soon after his return, he was snapped up by film director Raymond Chow to star in two movies. It was Lee's third film, *Way of the Dragon* (1972), with its legendary fight scenes with Chuck Norris, that ensured Lee's immortality as the world's most influential martial arts star. Hollywood finally accorded him the respect he sought in 1973, when he was cast as the star in *Enter the Dragon*, which catapulted him to global stardom. Despite his exceptional levels of fitness, Lee died suddenly, shortly before the film was released, which only accentuated his status as a cultural icon.

Left: Bruce Lee, in a scene from his iconic movie, *Enter the Dragon.*

Vivien Leigh

Born Vivian Mary Hartley
November 5, 1913
Darjeeling, India

Died July 7, 1967
London, England

Vivien Leigh was a classically beautiful English actress, best known for her marriage to Laurence Olivier and her electrifying performances in two of Hollywood's legendary movies, *Gone with the Wind* (1939) and *A Streetcar Named Desire* (1951).

Leigh's delicate beauty and classic English rose looks hid a fragile personality, blighted by bipolar disorder, which gave her a reputation as a 'difficult' star. Born in Darjeeling, India, where her father was an officer in the Indian cavalry, Leigh was educated in Europe, before enrolling at RADA (the Royal Academy of Dramatic Art) in London to train as an actress.

Aged only 19, Leigh was married, in 1932, to Herbert Leigh Holman, a barrister 13 years her senior, and gave up her dramatic ambitions to devote herself to her husband. However, she found domesticity restrictive and got a small part in an English film, *Things are Looking Up*, in 1935. Rejecting her agent's suggestion of the name April Morn, Vivian took the stage name Vivien Leigh, just altering the spelling of her first name. Having received good reviews for her role in the comedy *The Mask of Virtue* in London's West End, Leigh was spotted by Laurence Olivier. Their friendship developed into a full-blown affair on the set of *Fire Over England* (1937), their first movie together.

The professional pairing of Leigh and Olivier was a powerful one, with Leigh undoubtedly benefiting from Olivier's depth of understanding and great dramatic experience. They appeared together on the London stage, where Leigh was a frequent performer, before Olivier left for Hollywood in 1938. Leigh followed him, partly because she harbored

tenacious ambitions to be cast as Scarlett O'Hara in the forthcoming *Gone with the Wind*. She was a surprising choice for the role, being relatively inexperienced, as well as English, but she gave the performance of her life as Scarlett. She won the Oscar for Best Actress, married Olivier in 1940 and became one half of the most celebrated couple in Hollywood.

She worked with Olivier in a number of films and plays throughout the 1940s, but struggled with both mental and physical health problems. Casting Leigh in the 1949 London stage production of *A Streetcar Named Desire* was contentious, because of the disturbing nature of the play. But her exhilarating performance allowed her to repeat the role in the film adaptation, opposite Marlon Brando in 1951, which won her a second Oscar.

In later years, Leigh said her role as Blanche DuBois 'tipped me over into madness' and the episodes of depression certainly became more frequent during the 1950s.

Divorced from Olivier in 1960, Leigh continued to work occasionally in the theatre and in film and died of tuberculosis in 1967, at the age of 53.

Below: Leigh played Blanche Dubois to great acclaim in the stage production of *A Streetcar Named Desire* in London in 1949.

Right: Leigh in her most famous role, as the spoilt southern belle, Scarlett O'Hara, in *Gone with the Wind*.

Madonna

Born Madonna Louise
Veronica Ciccone
August 16, 1958
Bay City, Michigan, USA

Singer Madonna's ever-changing image has made for one of the most interesting careers in rock history.

The best-selling female rock artist of the 20th century, she has never shied away from controversy, often exploiting it simply to promote her work. The popularity of her music, her ability to embrace and often start new trends, as well as her astute business sense, have given her a degree of influence in the music industry unusual for any female artist.

Originally intending to become a dancer, Madonna turned to music and signed with Sire records in 1982, releasing her debut single *Everybody* the same year.

Her first album, *Madonna*, appeared in 1983 and produced a couple of chart singles. But it was her smash hit 1984 album, *Like a Virgin*, that established her image and shot the 'Material Girl' on to the world stage. Her next album, *True Blue* (1986), was a bestseller in 25 countries, producing three singles including the controversial *Papa Don't Preach*. The first female artist fully to exploit the power of music videos, she used them to give her songs an added visual punch as she explored religious symbolism and sexual themes in her work. *Like a Prayer*, released in 1989, received widespread critical acclaim and predictably, in view of the images of burning crosses in the video, condemnation from the Vatican.

The spectacular 'Blonde Ambition' tour of 1990 was a visual feast of provocative choreography and superlative music that delighted fans. Keen to have complete creative control over her work, Madonna founded her own entertainment company, Maverick, in 1992 and published her first book of photography, starkly entitled *Sex*, which was preceded by the album *Erotica*.

Perhaps surprised that her deliberately edgy work did not attract more favorable reviews, she appeared to mellow in the mid-1990s, as she paused to have her first child, daughter Lourdes.

Madonna has periodically branched out into film, appearing in some 20 movies, with mixed results. One of her earliest, *Desperately Seeking Susan* (1985), was a hit, but the following year *Shanghai Surprise* (with first husband Sean Penn) flopped. Probably her most successful role was as Eva Perón in the musical *Evita*, which won her a Golden Globe award in 1996. Her concerts and tours, however, have broken box office records, with her 2008 'Sticky and Sweet' tour grossing $280 million – more than any other tour by a solo artist.

Madonna divorced her second husband, Guy Ritchie and then apparently took up with a man 28 years her junior, called Jesus. But after nearly 30 years in the business, the 'Queen of Pop' retains her capacity to thrill and surprise her fans. Feisty, opinionated and hugely talented, Madonna continues to turn out the fantastic pop records that have made her the most successful female recording artist of all time.

Left: Always an exciting live performer, Madonna plays in Rome, 2008, during her 'Sticky and Sweet' tour.

Right: 'Blonde Ambition' – Madonna's provocative 1990 tour, which was slated by the Catholic church, but highly praised by musical critics.

Marcel Marceau

Born Marcel Mangel
March 22, 1923
Strasbourg, France

Died Died September 27, 2007
Cahors, France

Marceau's extraordinary career as the most famous mime artist in the world began not in the circus, or on the stage, but while working as a member of the French Resistance during World War II.

Born in Strasbourg, France, the son of a Jewish butcher, Marcel Mangel and his family changed their name to Marceau to escape the attention of the occupying German authorities during the second World War. Marcel and his brother joined the Resistance and it was to keep young Jewish children quiet, while they were escaping from the Nazis, that he used his miming skills. After the liberation of Paris in 1944, Marceau worked as a liaison officer for the French army, working with the American forces.

Shortly after he was demobilized, he enrolled at Charles Dullin's School of Dramatic Art in Paris and studied under the great mime master, Etienne Decroux. While still a student, he was inspired by the work of his great hero, Charlie Chaplin, to invent the character of Bip the Clown, a perennially doleful, white-faced clown, clad in a striped sweater, with a battered silk opera hat. Named for Pip in Dickens' *Great Expectations*, Bip epitomized the innocent alone in a world that was both terrifying and amazing and like Chaplin's Little Tramp, he was both downtrodden and rebellious.

Bip was to remain Marceau's most famous creation. Perhaps as a result of his wartime experiences, Marceau was a great believer in the strength of the human spirit. ' We know that the fighting spirit of man is everlasting,' he explained: 'Death is absurd, but humanity has to be eternal.' Marceau appeared as Bip on stage and on screen around the world for over 50 years, but it was his theatrical work that was most successful, as he performed most strongly in front of live audiences.

He established the Compagnie de Mime Marcel Marceau in 1949 and first toured the US in 1955. In New York, his show had to be moved from the Phoenix Theatre

to the Barrymore, a much larger venue, to accommodate the huge audiences. Aiming to spread 'L'art du silence' (the art of silence), Marceau became immensely popular in the US, where he made many television appearances. He undertook 40 world tours, the last one in 2006, shortly before he died. Marceau was showered with honors, notably the Légion d'honneur in France and was also widely known for his humanitarian work with the United Nations.

A delightful and charming interviewee, Marceau told journalists, 'Never get a mime talking. He won't stop.' But his ability to convey complex tales and emotions in silent gestures elevated mime to a highly regarded art form and influenced a new generation of entertainers. Michael Jackson's 'moonwalk' was probably inspired by Marceau and Rowan Atkinson's Mr Bean character undoubtedly owes a debt to him.

Left and far left: Marceau drew his inspiration from the classical Pierrot clowns, as well as Charlie Chaplin's character, the Little Tramp. He performed all over the world to spread what he called 'the art of silence.'

Bob Marley

Born Robert Nesta Marley
February 6, 1945
St. Ann, Jamaica

Died May 11, 1981
Miami, Florida, USA

Bob Marley was the foremost reggae artist of his generation, a pioneering musician, who transported reggae from the Caribbean to the wider world stage.

Born in the rural parish of St. Ann, Jamaica, Marley was the son of Norval Marley, a Jamaican Royal Marine officer of English descent and Cedella Booker, a young Afro-Jamaican. He left school at 14 and took himself off to Kingston to make music, meeting Neville 'Bunny' Livingston (later better known as Bunny Wailer) and Peter Tosh. Together they founded the Wailers, along with Junior Braithwaite, Cherry Smith and Beverley Kelso, in 1963. In 1964, their first single, *Simmer Down*, was a huge hit in Jamaica and they recorded some 20 singles, but with

the departure of Braithwaite and Kelso in 1965 and a lack of income, in 1966, the Wailers disbanded. Marley stayed with his mother in Newark, Delaware, working in a factory, before returning to Jamaica in 1967, where he became a devout Rastafarian.

The Wailers reunited and under the guidance of Lee 'Scratch' Perry, from 1969 recorded popular local hits, but the Jamaican record industry simply did not have the money, or influence to launch acts on to the international scene. The Wailers finally got a break when Chris Blackwell signed them to Island Records and with the release of their first album, *Catch a Fire*, in 1973, they got the international recognition

they so richly deserved. *Burnin'*, issued in 1974, included the hit *I Shot the Sheriff*, which was covered by Eric Clapton, raising Marley's profile still further. Having made an overseas tour in 1973, the Wailers disbanded in 1974, with Tosh and Livingston embarking on solo careers.

With a changed line-up that now included his wife, Rita, Marley continued to perform with the Wailers and toured Europe, Africa and the Americas. The outstanding track on their next album, *Natty Dread* (1974), was the soul-reggae ballad *No Woman, No Cry*, probably Marley's most popular song and his first

Top 40 hit in the UK. With a particularly loyal fan base in Britain, the Wailers had further hits with *Exodus* (1977), *Jamming* (1977) and *Is This Love* (1978).

Following a regular pattern of an album a year, followed by a concert tour, Marley established himself as an international star at the end of the 1970s, but his heart and his roots remained in Jamaica. He took new inspiration from Africa, after touring Gabon in 1978, which was reflected in his 1979 album *Survival*. Such was his status, that he was invited to perform at Zimbabwe's independence celebrations in 1980.

Just as he had succeeded in establishing reggae as more than just a minority music, Marley died from cancer at the tragically early age of 36. Revered, loved and admired, he was given a state funeral in Jamaica.

Left: Marley, with his characteristic dreadlocks, performing in 1978.

Below: Marley (center) flanked by Bunny Wailer and Peter Tosh, in 1964, the year of their first hit.

Steve McQueen

Born Terence Steven McQueen
March 24, 1930
Beech Grove, Indiana,
USA

Died November 7, 1980
Ciudad Juárez,
Chihuahua, Mexico

Actor Steve McQueen cultivated the image of a laconic loner, a tough, capable anti-hero, who could handle himself in a fight. At the height of his fame, he was known as 'the King of Cool.'

McQueen's on-screen persona was not so far from his real personality. He had an unstable upbringing, after his stunt pilot father left his mother to bring up their baby son alone. Partially deaf and dyslexic, Steve was an unsettled, rebellious teenager, who spent a year in reform school. When he left, aged 16, he went from job to job, before joining the Marines in 1947. In 1950, he drifted into acting, studying at the Neighborhood Playhouse in New York and funding his education by competing in weekend motorcycle races. Racing cars and motorcycles became an abiding passion and if he got the chance to drive in a movie, he tried to perform all his own stunts – insurance concerns permitting.

McQueen's career took off in 1958, when he won the part of bounty hunter Josh Randall on CBS TV's *Wanted: Dead or Alive*. Although he had already appeared on Broadway and in several films, it was *Wanted* that made him a household name. Director John Sturges recognized his potential and cast him in two of his best-known films, *The*

Magnificent Seven (1960) and *The Great Escape* (1963). The iconic motorcycle leap of the escaping prisoner-of-war in *The Great Escape* is one of McQueen's best-known screen moments, although he freely admitted that it was performed by Bud Ekins, his stunt double.

Firmly established as one of Hollywood's hottest properties, McQueen went on to star with Natalie Wood in *Love with the Proper Stranger* (1963) and earned his only Oscar nomination for his role in *The Sand Pebbles* (1966). One of his best-known movies, *Bullitt* (1968), with its amazing car chase through the streets of San Francisco, returned McQueen to the action hero role, starring alongside Jacqueline Bisset and Robert Vaughn. Once again, McQueen performed most of the driving stunts, combining his love of fast cars with his love of acting.

By 1972, when he starred in *The Getaway* with Ali MacGraw (who became his second wife in 1973), McQueen was the highest paid actor in the world. His role in *Papillon* in 1973, as a convict in a penal colony, hinted at his fine qualities as a character actor, though he returned firmly to action hero type in the disaster movie *The Towering Inferno* in 1974.

One of the great action stars of the 1960s and 1970s, McQueen never forgot his roots and throughout his career, supported the Boys Republic reform school that had turned him around in his teens.

Left: Although he once said, 'I'm not quite sure acting is something for a grown man to be doing,' Steve McQueen enjoyed his job.

Below: The classic image from *The Great Escape*.

Freddie Mercury

Born Farrokh Bulsara
September 5, 1946
Stone Town, Zanzibar

Died November 24, 1991
London, England

The theatrical and charismatic singer-songwriter, Freddie Mercury, was one of rock's greatest performers, a man who could hold an audience in the palm of his hand.

The most ostentatious member of a flamboyant band, Mercury combined an extraordinary singing voice with an endless capacity to entertain. Queen were formed at the height of the glam rock era and the group initially played up to the over-the-top image they created. However, their intelligence and talents were such that, fronted by Mercury, Queen transformed themselves into one of the great British rock supergroups of the 1970s and 1980s.

Freddie Mercury was born in Zanzibar and his family moved to Britain in 1964. Freddie joined several bands in the late 1960s, finally linking up with guitarist Brian May and drummer Roger Taylor in 1970 to form Queen. Bassist John Deacon was recruited the following year and Freddie changed his surname from Bulsara to Mercury.

The group spent much of the next two years rehearsing, while the band members also pursued academic studies. In 1973, their first album, *Queen*, was released and they began touring. Influenced by prog rock groups, such as Led Zeppelin and in Freddie's case, the energizing performances of Liza Minnelli, Queen were an immediate hit. *Queen II* reached No. 2 in the British album charts. With *Sheer Heart Attack* (1974), the band broke into the American market. The album was hugely successful and the single, *Killer Queen*, was a hit on both sides of the Atlantic. Queen's material drew on a variety of influences, from

hard rock to folk-like vocal harmonies and although Mercury did not compose all their hits, he reveled in writing complex musical compositions. The best example of these is Queen's most famous single, *Bohemian Rhapsody*, from the 1975 album *A Night at the Opera*. It was a ground-breaking song and stayed at the top of the British charts for two months. Six minutes long and in three distinct parts, it was accompanied by what is seen as the first music video in pop history. Later massive Queen hits, written by Mercury, included *Somebody to Love* and *We Are the Champions*.

By the late 1970s and into the 1980s, Queen concerts had become elaborate stadium rock affairs and Mercury was at the height of his performing powers. His live performances, epitomized by Queen's set at Live Aid in 1985, were theatrical, elaborate and involved the participation of thousands of delighted fans.

Mercury branched out with two solo albums in the 1980s, as well as an extraordinary collaboration with the Spanish opera singer Montserrat Caballé, *Barcelona* (1987). In the same year, he was diagnosed with AIDs, although this was not made public until the day before his death in 1991.

Mercury was one of a kind and although he was much imitated, few other singers shared his charisma, or dynamism.

Right: Queen were the ultimate stadium rock band and no one could manipulate a crowd of thousands quite as skillfully as Mercury.

Below: Mercury on stage in Rio de Janeiro, 1985.

George Michael

A confident and assured musician, George Michael has enjoyed a tremendously successful pop career, first as one half of the 1980s pop duo Wham! and subsequently as a solo performer.

Born in north London, to a Greek Cypriot father and English mother, George began writing and performing his own music with school friend, Andrew Ridgeley. They formed their first band, The Executive, in 1981. Quickly realizing that they were stronger as a duo, Ridgeley and Michael formed Wham! later that year.

The combination of their youthful good looks, carefree lifestyle and infectiously snappy musical compositions soon got them the publicity they craved. In 1982 their first single, *Wham Rap*, got to No. 8 in the British charts and was swiftly followed by *Young Guns (Go For It)*. Further singles from their second album, *Make It Big*, released in 1984, made it to the top of the charts, notably *Wake Me Up Before You Go-Go* and *Freedom*, along with *Careless Whisper*, released as a solo single by Michael. Wham! became the latest teenage pop sensation, but in spite of their success, by 1986, Michael wanted to move on to a more sophisticated sound and Wham! disbanded.

Michael's first solo album, *Faith*, released in 1987, showcased a new, more serious talent. Gone were the disposable pop tunes, to be replaced by mature, funky, soul-driven ballads (all except one written by Michael himself) that sent the album to No. 1 on both sides of the Atlantic. He had four No. 1 singles from the album: *Faith*, *Father Figure*, *One More Try* and *Monkey*, while the slightly controversial *I Want Your Sex* hit No. 2. With a Grammy and two Ivor Novello awards under his belt, not to mention some 16 million sales, Michael was taken extremely seriously by the musical establishment.

Michael's rugged image of designer stubble, shades and black leather appealed to a broad spectrum of fans, but after the successful release of *Listen Without Prejudice Vol. 1* in 1990, Michael terminated his contract with Sony, partly because he disliked being marketed as a sex symbol. *Older* (1996) marked a new departure, with a marked jazz influence and melancholy tone: George's life had been troubled – he had been engaged in legal wrangling with his record company and his life partner, Anselmo Feleppa, had died – and these issues undoubtedly affected his music. In 1998, he hit the headlines, when he was arrested in Los Angeles for 'engaging in a lewd act', although he later made a joke of the incident in his single, *Outside*.

With the release of *Twenty Five* in 2006, Michael celebrated 25 years in pop and began his first European tour in 15 years. His popularity in the UK has never diminished, with all his albums reaching the No. 1, or No. 2 spot, a remarkable achievement for any performer.

Born Georgios Kyriacos Panayiotou
June 25, 1963
London, England

Left: Michael projected a more mature image during his early years as a solo artist.

Below: Michael on stage during Wham!'s tour of the USA, 1985. In April that year, Wham! toured China, the first western group to perform there.

Mickey Mouse

Created November 18, 1928
Los Angeles, California, USA

Mickey Mouse was the first and arguably the greatest international cartoon character created during the 20th century. Instantly recognizable, with his round black ears, red shorts and pert snout, Mickey was the creation of Walt Disney, the animation genius known as 'the man behind the mouse.'

Since his creation in 1928, Mickey has become an icon, not only of the Disney Company, but also of the USA – a cultural symbol of America recognized around the world. Inspired by the pet he kept as a child, Disney dreamed up the idea of a cute mouse character, who was originally christened Mortimer Mouse. Drawn by Disney's long-time collaborator Ub Iwerks, Mickey (renamed by Disney's wife, Lillian) featured in two poorly received short animations, before appearing in his first talkie, *Steamboat Willie*, in November 1928. With sound movies only a year old, audiences were thrilled to hear sound used in an animated cartoon feature and Mickey was voiced by Disney himself, who had succeeded in taking advantage of the popular new technology.

Iwerks and Disney parted company in 1930, but Mickey lived on, as other animators were recruited to draw him. During the lean Depression years, Mickey became immensely popular, starring in a string of short animated features, in a variety of anthropomorphic roles, but rarely as an actual mouse. Initially black and white, Mickey did not appear in color until 1935.

In 1930, the Mickey Mouse comic strip was syndicated to newspapers across the USA, with the first strips drawn by Ub Iwerks. After he had left and another artist had quickly moved on, Walt Disney asked a third artist, Floyd Gottfredson, to take over temporarily. He continued to draw the strip for the next 45 years until he retired in 1975.

Mickey starred in over 120 different animated cartoons, alongside a family of characters – Minnie, Goofy, Pluto, Donald Duck and others. His success lay in his versatility – he could appear as anything, in any walk of life. Mischievous, courageous, romantic, misguided and often heroic, he was Everymouse and audiences loved him.

In 1932, Disney was awarded a special Academy Award for his creation, an honor that recognized the skill of his team of animators. On screen, Mickey has not aged, but he has been subtly altered over the years, notably, in *The Pointer* (1939), where animator, Fred Moore, gave Mickey's eyes pupils, to make them more expressive.

In the 1950s, Disney grasped the new challenges of television and from 1955 Mickey hosted *The Mickey Mouse Club*, which became the most successful children's show on television. Revived in the 1970s, the program was succeeded in 1999 by computer-animated educational shows for the Disney Channel – *Mickey Mouse Works*, Disney's *House of Mouse* and more recently, *Mickey Mouse Clubhouse*.

The amazing longevity of Disney's most popular creation is due to the universal charm of Mickey's character. Funny, cute, plucky, innocent and optimistic, he has appealed to the better side of human nature across the generations.

Right and below: Created in 1928, Mickey was quickly joined by a host of cartoon friends. Minnie first appeared in the short animation *Plane Crazy* in 1928 and the following year, in *Mickey's Follies*, it became clear that she was Mickey's girlfriend.

142

Kylie Minogue

Singer and actress, Kylie is one of a handful of entertainers universally known by her first name. Officially the most played female artist on UK radio, for two decades she has successfully marketed her own brand of immensely catchy pop.

Born in Melbourne, Kylie was a child actor in Australia, joining the cast of the soap opera *Neighbours* in 1986, as Charlene Robinson and playing opposite Jason Donovan. Their partnership was a crucial part of the show's success, in both Australia and Britain. Their screen wedding, in 1987, was watched by 20 million viewers in the UK, where Kylie's girl-next-door appeal won her millions of fans.

With her petite frame, outsized by her gutsy voice and showgirl charisma, Kylie seamlessly made the transition from soap superstar to global singing sensation in the late 1980s. In 1987, she became a part of the Stock, Aitken and Waterman hit-making machine, after releasing a cover version of the 1962 song *The Loco-Motion*, which became Australia's best-selling single of the 1980s. She recorded *I Should be So Lucky* that same year. An instant pop hit, the song reached No. 1 in the UK and Australia, while Kylie returned home to work on *Neighbours*. Her singing career began to outshine her acting after the release of her first album, *Kylie*, in 1988, which generated five Top Ten singles in Australia, the UK and parts of Europe.

Kylie's dance-pop music was popular, chart-topping and lucrative, but it was regarded rather snootily by music critics. In 1990, Kylie broke away from Stock, Aitken and Waterman to promote herself as a more mature, sexy artist, directing her own music videos and launching a new phase in her career. Influenced by musicians, such as Nick Cave and Michael Hutchence of INXS, Kylie became more creative. Her collaboration album, *Impossible Princess* (1997), became her most successful release since *Kylie* in 1988.

In the 1990s, Kylie appeared to be guided by more experienced members of the music business, but by the early 2000s no one could be in any doubt that she was in charge of her own career.

She acknowledged a (small) debt to Madonna in one interview: 'We both like to keep an eye on what's happening – trends. She's definitely the front-runner in this business, but I share her enthusiasm for being experimental ... And I've got a good commercial head on my shoulders.' In the early years of the new century, Kylie's stage acts became more extravagant, inspired by burlesque performances and Broadway musicals. The 'Showgirl' tour was interrupted by her successful treatment for breast cancer in 2005–6.

Kylie has shrewdly managed her image throughout her career and confounded critics with record sales and airplay that are the true testimony to her popularity around the world.

Born Kylie Ann Minogue
May 28, 1968
Melbourne, Victoria,
Australia

Left: Britain is home to some of Kylie's most devoted fans. Here she performs in Hyde Park, London, 2009.

Below: Kylie Minogue on stage at Le Bataclan in Paris, 2001.

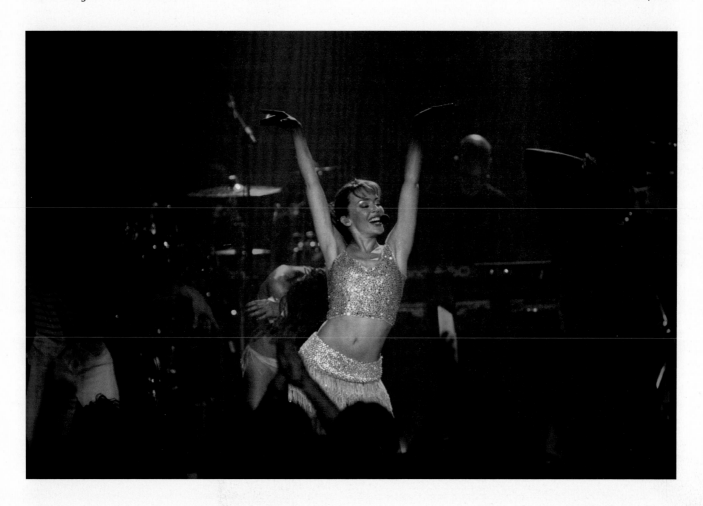

Marilyn Monroe

Born Norma Jeane Mortenson
June 1, 1926
Los Angeles, California,
USA

Died August 5, 1962
Los Angeles, California,
USA

The ultimate blonde bombshell, Hollywood glamour girl and confused victim, actress and singer Marilyn Monroe, had an appeal that glows as vividly today as it did in her short lifetime.

Born to an unstable mother and an unnamed runaway father, Marilyn spent much of her childhood in foster homes and orphanages, marrying for the first time at 16. She was talent-spotted by a photographer in 1944 and began her lifelong love affair with the camera as a model.

After two years, she signed her first studio contract with 20th Century Fox, dyed her hair blonde and changed her name. Her early film roles were unremarkable (as indeed were many of her later ones). She first attracted serious attention in 1950, in two minor and already typecast roles, first in John Huston's thriller *The Asphalt Jungle* as the gangster's luscious moll and then, in *All About Eve*, as a dim blonde among urban sophisticates. Fox recognized her screen potential and put her into a series of films in the early 1950s. *Tense Niagara,* the delightfully funny *Gentlemen Prefer Blondes* and *How to Marry a Millionaire* – all made in 1953 – together lifted her to superstardom. Her brief marriage to baseball star, Joe DiMaggio, dates from this time.

In 1955, determined to take control of her career and to master the stage fright that contributed to a reputation for unreliability, Monroe took a break from filming to study acting with Lee Strasberg in New York and *Bus Stop* (1956) proved that she could turn in a straight dramatic performance. The press had fun with her relationship at this time with famous playwright Arthur Miller, calling the pair 'the Egghead and the Hourglass.' They married in 1956 and for a time were ecstatically happy; Miller described her as 'a whirling light ... all paradox and mystery.' *Some Like It Hot* (1959) was a huge success, gaining Monroe a Golden Globe award, although it relegated her to 'dumb blonde' status again. Miller wrote the screenplay of *The Misfits* (1960) as a gift for her, but by the time the film was shot, their marriage had fallen apart and Marilyn turned in a dispiriting performance.

If her screen roles are of variable quality, her musical numbers are enchanting – from *Diamonds are a Girl's Best Friend* in *Gentlemen Prefer Blondes* and *I Want to Be Loved by You* in *Some Like It Hot*, to *My Heart Belongs to Daddy* in Cukor's *Let's Make Love* (1960). It was her singing of 'Happy Birthday' at a party for President Kennedy in May 1962, that opened the last mysterious phase of her life, with allegations of affairs with both Jack and Bobby Kennedy. Popular doubt persists as to the real cause of her death, reportedly from a drug overdose, but her luminous beauty, feminine sensuality and allure, combined with a childlike vulnerability, have ensured her iconic status.

Right: Iconic and fabulous - Marilyn at her most glamorous, 1953.

Below: With John Huston (left) and husband Arthur Miller (right) on the set of her last movie, *The Misfits*.

Jim Morrison

Born James Douglas Morrison
December 8, 1943
Melbourne, Florida, USA

Died July 3, 1971
Paris, France

Singer, songwriter, poet and Sixties wild child, Jim Morrison was the prototype of the gifted and troubled rock star. As lead singer and lyricist of the psychedelic rock band, The Doors, his charismatic, scandalous and unpredictable performances made rock history.

Morrison had an itinerant childhood, as his father was a career US Navy officer, but by 1964, he had moved to the West Coast of America and was studying film at UCLA. After graduating, he led a bohemian intellectual life, hanging out with writers and journalists in Venice Beach, reading Nietzsche, Rimbaud and Kerouac and writing poetry. In 1965, he formed The Doors with former fellow student and keyboardist, Ray Manzarek and they were soon joined by drummer, John Densmore and guitarist, Robby Krieger. They took the band's name from the title of a book by Aldous Huxley, about his experiences with the drug mescaline, *The Doors of Perception*, which in turn was a quote from visionary poet, William Blake. Both the poetic and the drug links were to prove fundamental for Morrison.

In June 1966, The Doors played the prestigious Whisky a Go Go club on Sunset Boulevard, as support group for Van Morrison's band, Them. Jim's developing stage persona, with its recklessness and air of menace, was influenced by Van Morrison. The band signed to Elektra in 1966 and their first album, *The Doors*, included their first hit single *Light My Fire*, which made the No. 1 slot on the Billboard singles chart and sold over a million copies. The song was largely written by Krieger – the band collaborated on many of their lyrics – but it was Morrison's baritone voice and the dark-edged

eroticism of his performance that caught public attention. The famous 'Young Lion' photo session in 1967 immortalized Morrison in his rock icon role.

The Doors' next album, *Strange Days* (1967), featured more of Morrison's elliptical, wide-ranging, pseudo-poetic lyrics, including the title track, which reflected on the emerging hippy youth culture and *People are Strange*, about alienation. His own alienation was growing stronger and more troublesome. He would turn up late for live performances or drunk for recordings and the band took a lengthy break in 1969, before recording the last album that Morrison made, *LA Woman*.

Meanwhile Morrison had self-published two volumes of poetry and recorded some of his poems in a professional sound studio. In a performance in Louisiana, to

publicize *LA Woman*, Morrison appeared to have a breakdown on stage, refusing to perform for the rest of the gig and his fellow musicians decided to cut short the live act.

Morrison moved to Paris, apparently intending to become a writer in exile, like so many of his heroes, but within three months he was dead, probably from a heroin overdose.

Left: Wild and charismatic, Morrison thrilled fans.

Below: The Doors in LA, 1969. They were one of the most controversial rock acts of the 1960s, partly because of Morrison's unpredictable behavior.

Paul Newman

Born Paul Leonard Newman
January 26, 1925
Cleveland, Ohio, USA

Died September 26, 2008
Westport, Connecticut,
USA

The ultimate all-American blue-eyed boy, Paul Newman was the great Hollywood survivor, whose charisma and talent secured him substantial roles, throughout a film career spanning over 50 years.

A much acclaimed actor, with one Oscar for Scorsese's *The Color of Money* (1986) and eight nominations, he was also a film director, philanthropist, entrepreneur, car-race enthusiast and unusually for Hollywood, devoted family man.

Born to parents who ran a sporting goods store, Newman showed an early interest in the theater. After naval service, in the Pacific during World War II, he studied drama at Yale and with Lee Strasberg in New York, making his Broadway debut in 1953.

The first Hollywood role followed almost immediately and in 1955, he landed the part of boxer, Rocky Graziano, in *Somebody Up There Likes Me*. The part, originally intended for James Dean, established his film persona as the tough kid who makes good. In 1957, a landmark year, he won a Golden Globe for Most Promising Newcomer and began his lifelong relationship with actor Joanne Woodward – they met on the set of *The Long Hot Summer* and married a year later. *Cat on a Hot Tin Roof* with Elizabeth Taylor (1958), based on the play by Tennessee Williams, gave him the chance to turn in a more subtle performance, as the neurotic alcoholic, Brick and earned him his first Oscar nomination.

Newman was one of a minority of screen idols from the last days of the 1950s star system, who remained a box office draw in the grittier movies of the 1960s and 1970s. His rebellious screen persona, allied with his personal charm, led to a stream of good parts, beginning with perhaps his most memorable role of all, the cocky pool shark in the downbeat atmospheric drama *The Hustler* (1961). *Hud* (1964), *Cool Hand Luke* (1967) and *The Life and Times of Judge Roy Bean* (1972) all played to the tough-guy image, while his two classic films with Robert Redford, *Butch Cassidy and the Sundance Kid* (1969) and *The Sting* (1973), added charm and humor, to make an irresistible package.

Newman also directed several feature films, some of them starring his wife, Joanne Woodward, such as the Oscar-nominated *Rachel, Rachel* (1968) and *The Glass Menagerie* (1987). At the same time, Newman was indulging his taste for auto racing, winning at Thompson, Connecticut, in 1972 and coming second at Le Mans, France, in 1979. Meanwhile, the parts kept rolling in, with *The Towering Inferno* (1974), *The Verdict* (1982), *The Color of Money* – in which he reprised his hustler character – and his Oscar-nominated Irish mobster in *Road to Perdition* (2002). His food company, founded as a charitable concern in the 1980s, became a million dollar business. When his death (from lung cancer) was announced, every theater on Broadway dimmed its lights, in tribute to one of their own.

Left: Newman on the set of *Hud*, 1962, for which he won an Oscar nomination.

Right: *Fort Apache – the Bronx* was a huge success at the time of its release in 1981, largely due to Newman's performance.

Jack Nicholson

Charismatic film actor Jack Nicholson has an extraordinary Oscar record, with nominations in every decade since the 1960s.

In a sequence of landmark roles, in films from the brilliant *One Flew Over the Cuckoo's Nest* (1975), through *The Shining* (1980) and *The Witches of Eastwick* (1987), to *Batman* (1989), Nicholson has created a classic screen persona, as the droll, enigmatic, contradictory – and sometimes dangerous – non-conformist, reveling in the opportunity to cause havoc.

Nicholson was brought up to believe that his mother was his sister and his grandparents his parents. He soon moved to Los Angeles, where he started out in low-budget films in the 1950s. He finally made his mark – and won his first Oscar nomination – with a support role, as the hard-drinking lawyer in the road movie *Easy Rider* (1969), while his subtle and nuanced performance as the dogged private eye in Chinatown (1974) made him a star. *One Flew Over the Cuckoo's Nest* might well not have been made without Nicholson's status and support, together with his willingness to act in an ensemble. The result was well-deserved Oscars for star, film, script and director, but his wonderfully over-the-top characterization of the irrepressibly subversive McMurphy led to some limiting and typecast roles and a tendency to self-parody.

Born John Joseph Nicholson
April 22, 1937
New York City, or
Neptune, New Jersey, USA
(sources differ)

The 1980s, though, saw some more challenging parts. In Warren Beatty's epic *Reds* (1981), Nicholson turned in a controlled (and Oscar-nominated) performance, as the remote, but romantic playwright, Eugene O'Neill and his touchingly boisterous ex-astronaut who courts Shirley MacLaine in *Terms of Endearment* (1983), was an Oscar winner. After his wonderfully dim Mafia hitman in *Prizzi's Honor* (1985), playing opposite long-term girlfriend, Anjelica Huston, Nicholson returned to wildly funny outrageousness, as the sinister Daryl Van Horne in *The Witches of Eastwick*. The revelation that he was expecting a child with actress and model, Rebecca Broussard, ended the relationship with Huston.

The mix of serious acting and bombastic role play continued to characterize Nicholson's roles into the 1990s. Yet another Oscar nomination came for his commanding officer covering up a murder in *A Few Good Men* (1992). He neatly combined the serious and comedic in *Wolf* (1994), as a book editor, who turns into a werewolf, with a convincingly low-key performance.

More recent roles have been quieter, more reflective, even sadder and Nicholson has mostly chosen to work with old friends. His sharp performance as the curmudgeonly author, who falls for single mother Helen Hunt in *As Good as It Gets* (1997) won him a third Oscar, while his understated and sympathetic playing of a widowed salesman in *About Schmidt* (2002) earned him a 12th nomination, breaking his own record as the most nominated male actor in Oscar history.

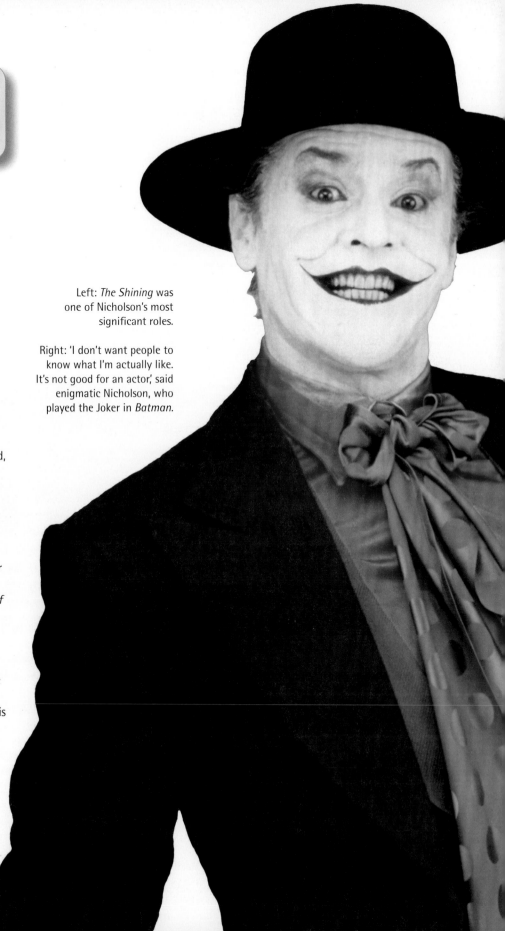

Left: *The Shining* was one of Nicholson's most significant roles.

Right: 'I don't want people to know what I'm actually like. It's not good for an actor,' said enigmatic Nicholson, who played the Joker in *Batman*.

Barack Obama

Born Barack Hussein Obama
August 4, 1961
Honolulu, Hawaii, USA

American lawyer, author and politician, Barack Obama made history by becoming the first African-American president of the USA in January 2009.

Born in Honolulu, to a black African father from Kenya and a white American mother from Kansas, Obama moved, in 1967, with his mother to Indonesia, returning to Honolulu to live with his grandparents in 1971, for his schooling. He later wrote of the value of his experience in Hawaii, where a variety of cultures interacted in a climate of mutual respect. He went on to college in Los Angeles and then studied at Columbia University, New York, graduating in political science.

In 1985, Obama made a career-defining move to Chicago, to work in public service, as a community organizer on the tough South Side. Moving to Harvard Law School in 1988, he gained national attention (and the offer of a book contract, for the celebrated *Dreams From My Father*, published in 1995) by becoming the first black president of the *Harvard Law Review*. He continued to work in Chicago each summer, meeting his future wife, Michelle Robinson, at this time and returned there in 1991 to teach constitutional law at the University of Chicago and to join a small civil rights law firm.

Obama ran successfully for a seat in the Illinois Senate in 1996, where he championed social welfare reforms. He first ran (unsuccessfully) for Congress in

2000, but in 2004, stunned the Illinois Democrats with an emphatic win, against six challengers, in the state primary to select a Senate candidate. In July 2004, he seemed to have come from nowhere, when he delivered an electrifying keynote address at the Democratic National Convention. 'The Audacity of Hope' was instantly dubbed one of the best keynote speeches of the modern era. Suddenly, he was viewed as a possible leader, even a possible president and he won his Senate seat a few months later, with 70 per cent of the vote.

Obama's presidential campaign, beginning in February 2007, broke numerous records. In an eventual two-horse race, he beat Hillary Clinton to gain the Democratic presidential nomination in 2008. He clinched the presidential election with 53 per cent of the popular vote, against John McCain's 46 per cent, to become the USA's 44th president.

The first months of the Obama presidency were overshadowed by global economic crisis. In February 2009, a $787 billion economic stimulus package aided recovery, while GM and Chrysler, both huge employers, were bailed out. Clear indicators of a massive policy shift included the announcement of the closure of Guantanamo Bay detention center, a timetable for the withdrawal of US forces from Iraq, restrictions lifted on stem cell research and a proactive engagement with foreign policy issues, particularly the Middle East. The passing of a (much fought over) healthcare bill in January 2010 and the announcement of a nuclear limitation agreement with Russia in March, made for a productive first year in office.

Left and overleaf: Obama said, 'I stand here knowing that my story is part of the larger American story . . . and that in no other country on Earth is my story even possible.' His rise to power is the embodiment of the American dream.

Below: With his family on Inauguration Day, January 2009.

155

Laurence Olivier

Born Laurence Kerr Olivier
May 22, 1907
Dorking, Surrey, England

Died July 11, 1989
Steyning, West Sussex,
England

Acclaimed English actor, director and co-founder of the National Theatre in London, Laurence Olivier was one of the most revered actors of his generation on both stage and screen. In his long career he played everything from the heroic king in Shakespeare's *Henry V* (1944) to the terrifying villain with dentist's drill in *Marathon Man* (1976).

The young actor's stage breakthrough came in 1930, in the London production of Noël Coward's *Private Lives*. By 1931 he was in Hollywood, playing the romantic lead. Film was not his preferred medium, however and he was soon back on stage in England, alternating the roles of Romeo and Mercutio with his professional rival, John Gielgud, in Shakespeare's *Romeo and Juliet* (1935). This led to a series of star Shakespearean roles for impresario Lilian Baylis, at the Old Vic Theatre in London, where his roles included Henry V, Coriolanus, Iago and Hamlet, the latter opposite Vivien Leigh, as Ophelia.

When Olivier returned to Hollywood to play Heathcliff in *Wuthering Heights* (1939), Leigh soon followed to make her successful bid to play Scarlett O'Hara in *Gone With the Wind*. The success of both movies, with Olivier nominated for and Leigh winning an Oscar, made them both international celebrities. Olivier's next two films, both made in 1940, were classics – Hitchcock's *Rebecca* and *Pride and Prejudice*, with Greer Garson. Olivier and Vivien Leigh were married the same year.

World War II saw the couple back in England, with Olivier training as a pilot and serving two years in the Fleet Air Arm. In 1944, he was released from service to form a new Old Vic Theatre Company, performing a whole series of classic and modern plays to eager wartime and postwar audiences. He also directed his first film, *Henry V*, a glorious flight of fancy which starts within the confines of Shakespeare's Globe Theatre and takes wing into film. He went on to direct films of *Hamlet* (1948) and *Richard III* (1955).

Olivier's principal postwar commitment was to the long-planned National Theatre, of which he was co-founder and inaugural director. He opened in *Hamlet* (1963) and during the ten years of his directorship, acted in 12 plays and directed nine. Film-making at this time proved a welcome distraction and then became a necessity, when his marriage to Joan Plowright, in 1962, produced three children to support. He received Oscar nominations for his roles in the ingenious thriller *Sleuth* (1972), *Marathon Man* and *The Boys from Brazil* (1978).

Olivier was knighted in 1947. In 1970, he became the first actor to be created a life peer and in 1984, the Laurence Olivier Awards (for London theatre productions) were named in his honor. However, he always preferred to be addressed not as Sir Laurence, or Lord Olivier, but simply as Larry.

Left: *Henry V,* produced during World War II as a morale-boosting film, was one of Olivier's finest roles.

Below: Olivier won his tenth Oscar nomination for his role in *The Boys from Brazil.*

Jacqueline Kennedy Onassis

> **Born** Jacqueline Lee Bouvier
> July 28, 1929
> Southampton, New York,
> USA
>
> **Died** May 19, 1994
> New York, USA

First Lady, stunning beauty and fashion icon, Jackie Kennedy revitalized the White House during her husband's cruelly curtailed presidency and permanently changed the public perception of the First Lady's role.

Born into a comfortably wealthy and well-established New York family, Jackie had a traditional upbringing and made her society debut in 1947, when she was named Debutante of the Year. She was also smart and artistic, attending Vassar College and spending a student year in Grenoble, France. She married the then Senator, John F. 'Jack' Kennedy, in 1953, two years after graduating.

The marriage of these two clever, gifted and beautiful people looked to be made in heaven. The early years were tough, however, with Jackie suffering first a miscarriage and then a stillbirth, before their daughter Caroline was born in 1957. Meanwhile, Jack was often ill and already indulging his notorious penchant for affairs.

When the White House beckoned, Jackie showed both her style and her steel. Though pregnant throughout the 1960 presidential campaign (John junior was born two weeks after the election), she hired a politically astute social secretary to advise her and regularly accompanied her husband on the campaign trail. Shocked by the rundown state of the presidential residence, she determined to make it both a comfortable family home and a showcase for American history and talent. Initially drawing criticism at the cost, this move came to be understood as a brilliant statement of a new era. In February 1962, Jackie led a nationally televised tour of the White House and it became a new and regular venue for cultural performances by US companies.

Jackie was concerned, at the same time, to guard the privacy of her children and appeared infrequently in public, though making a point of getting it right when she did. In her pillbox hats, Chanel suits and elegantly comfortable flat shoes, she influenced a generation of women. When the Kennedys visited France in 1962, she charmed the French with her style, ease of manner and command of their language – JFK ruefully described himself as 'the man who accompanied Jacqueline Kennedy to France.'

The year of JFK's death had already been a tragic one for the couple, as their son, Patrick, died two days after his birth in August. After the bleak November day in Dallas, when her husband was killed, Jackie impressed the world with her stoicism, dignity and courage.

Her marriage to the Greek shipping magnate, Aristotle Onassis, in 1968, was less popular, but the assassination of Robert Kennedy six months earlier had left Jackie in fear for her children's safety and she wanted them out of the US. After Onassis' death in 1975, Jackie reinvented herself yet again, as a writer, editor and publisher, while continuing to work to preserve and protect America's cultural heritage.

Right: After the traumatic events of 1963, Jacqueline Kennedy demonstrated purposeful survival instincts. In 1975 she returned to New York for a successful publishing career.

Left: Graceful, elegant and beautiful, Kennedy was widely praised for her dignity in the wake of her husband's assassination.

161

Dolly Parton

Born Dolly Rebecca Parton
January 19, 1946
Sevierville, Tennessee,
USA

Blessed with a distinctive soprano and a deceptively 'dumb blonde' appearance, the 'Queen of Country Music' is one of the most successful female country music singers. She has had a record-breaking number of hits over her 50-year career.

The fourth of 12 children, Dolly Parton was raised in a one-room cabin in rural Tennessee, with music a fundamental part of her upbringing. As a child, she learned to play guitar and banjo and began to make up songs. Appearing regularly on a local radio variety show, she made her debut at the Grand Ole Opry in Nashville in 1958, aged 13. She moved to Nashville for good in 1964 and her first hit single was *Dumb Blonde*, which attracted the attention of country star, Porter Wagoner. He invited her to join his weekly syndicated television program and they

made an almost uninterrupted string of Top Ten singles together over the next six years.

Initially, Parton's solo efforts were less successful, but in 1970 *Joshua* finally made it to the No. 1 slot, followed closely by *Coat of Many Colors* (1971), which described her poverty-stricken childhood and swiftly became her signature tune and finally, *Jolene* (1974). That was also the year that she finally left Wagoner's show, writing the classic *I Will Always Love You* to commemorate the relationship. It was a measure of her business savvy that she refused Elvis Presley's request to cover the song, because it would have meant signing away half the rights. The song has made her millions and she earned the admiring title 'the Iron Butterfly'. Between 1974

and 1980, she had eight more No. 1 hits, winning a Grammy in 1977 for Best Female Country Vocal Performer.

Parton's big screen debut was in 1980, when she played a brassy Southerner in *Nine to Five,* opposite Jane Fonda and Lily Tomlin and won an Oscar nomination for the title song. Many more films have followed, including *Rhinestone* (1984), in which she sang a duet with Sylvestor Stallone and the star-studded *Steel Magnolias* (1989). In 1986, she established Dolly Parton Enterprises to control her growing empire and also began to support a number of charities, notably a drive to improve literacy, by distributing free books.

Meanwhile, the string of hit singles continued, with five No.1 solo hits between 1981 and 1984, plus her duet with Kenny Rogers, *Islands in the Stream.* Country fans were becoming critical of this more mainstream focus, but her album *Trio* (1987), with Linda Ronstadt and Emmylou Harris, re-established her as a true country singer and produced three Top Ten country singles.

The hit singles may have ended, but Parton's activities show no sign of slowing down. She published her autobiography in 1994, made another album with Ronstadt and Harris in 1999 and in 2008, released her first mainstream country album for 20 years, *Backwoods Barbie*.

Left: Dolly appeared with Porter Wagoner on his popular TV show from 1967 to 1974.

Right: Dolly admits she has had cosmetic surgery to maintain her voluptuous image.

Luciano Pavarotti

Born October 12, 1935
Modena, Italy

Died September 6, 2007
Modena, Italy

The Italian operatic tenor, Luciano Pavarotti, whose effortless voice, substantial presence and lovably roguish personality helped to demystify the world of high opera, was one of the most commercially successful tenors of all time.

Pavarotti's father was an amateur singer and though the young Luciano wanted initially to be a soccer star, he was soon singing with his father in a local church choir and studied music with childhood friend and future star soprano, Mirella Freni.

The turning point came in 1955 when his choir won first prize at the International Eisteddfod, a prestigious music competition in Wales. He began to train seriously as an operatic singer, making his national debut, in 1961, as Rodolfo in *La Bohème* in Reggio-Emilia and his international debut in Vienna, in the same role, two years later. This brought him to the attention of diva, Joan Sutherland, who wanted a tall tenor to accompany her on an Australian tour. At over 6 feet (1.9 m), Pavarotti fitted the bill nicely and they sang over 40 performances in two months. Pavarotti later credited Sutherland with teaching him the breathing technique that sustained his long career.

Well-received debuts at La Scala, Milan and the Royal Opera House, London, followed. But it was at the Metropolitan Opera, New York, in 1972, that Pavarotti hit the big time, with his effortless performance of nine successive top notes in the role of Tonio in Donizetti's *La Fille du Régiment*, which earned him frenzied applause, 17 curtain calls and the title 'King of the High Cs'. From then on, he was hugely sought after, making

his Salzburg debut in 1976 and returning in *Idomoneo* in 1983. However, this success had its dark side. Pavarotti was an unreliable performer and became known as the 'King of Cancellations' for his habit of last-minute non-appearances.

Instead, he branched out from the world of opera on to the wider music scene. During a tour to China in 1986, 'Big Lucy' performed the first ever concert in the Great Hall of the People in Beijing, receiving yet another standing ovation. In 1990, his recording of *Nessun Dorma* from Puccini's *Turandot* was the theme song for the BBC's World Cup coverage, achieving top pop status. The Three Tenors – Pavarotti together with José Carreras and Plácido Domingo – made their first appearance on the eve of the World Cup final, producing the biggest selling classical recording of all time and helping to bring opera to a wider audience. Pavarotti also performed with Bono, Eric Clapton, Céline Dion and the Spice Girls and founded the International Pavarotti Voice

Competition, to support and encourage young singers.

His funeral was effectively a state occasion, with an aerobatic fly-past, a farewell message on the Juventus FC website and a CNN broadcast.

Left and below: Pavarotti's amazing tenor voice and larger than life personality enabled him to straddle the divide between classical opera and popular music.

Pelé

Born Edison Arantes do Nascimento
October 23, 1940
Três Corações, Brazil

Always known by his nickname, the Brazilian footballer, Pelé, is arguably the greatest – and best loved – player of all time.

A national hero in Brazil and the all-time lead scorer for the national football team, Pelé is the only footballer to have played in three winning World Cup squads, the first aged just 17. It was Pelé who dubbed football 'the beautiful game.'

The son of a footballer, Pelé grew up in poverty in São Paolo and played with a local junior team. There, he was spotted by former Brazilian international Waldemar de Brito, who introduced him to professional football in Santos, a Brazilian industrial and port city. At 15, he joined the Santos FC junior team, moving to the first team in 1957 and becoming their top scorer, still aged only 16. Only ten months after he turned professional, Pelé was playing with the Brazilian national team, becoming the youngest player to score in international football, against Argentina.

The records continued to fall, as Pelé joined his first World Cup team in 1958, becoming the youngest player to do so, the youngest to score a goal (against Wales), the youngest to score a hat-trick (against France in the semi-final) and the youngest to play in a final (against Sweden). He scored two goals in the final, the first of them hailed as one of the best in the history of the World Cup and ended the tournament, having scored an astonishing six goals in four matches.

In the 1962 World Cup, Pelé played well in the first round, but was injured in the match against Czechoslovakia and had to miss the rest of the tournament,

though Brazil still won the title. The 1966 competition was a brutal contest, with Brazil knocked out in the first round and Pelé viciously fouled in two matches. He vowed, then, that this would be his last World Cup, but was persuaded otherwise in 1970, when he joined one of the strongest ever teams. In the final against Italy, he scored the opening goal – Brazil's 100th World Cup goal – with a header and Brazil went on to win 4–1.

Throughout his World Cup career, Pelé continued to play for Santos, although wealthy European clubs, such as Real Madrid, Juventus and Manchester United, all competed to sign him. This was no surprise, given his extraordinary lifetime record of 1,280 goals, when 400 is regarded as an achievement. In 1961, the Brazilian government declared him a 'national treasure', in order to prevent him being transferred abroad against his will.

Pelé's many nicknames are testimony to the hold he established on football fans everywhere – 'Gasoline' for his energy, the 'Executioner' for his finishing and the 'Black Pearl' for his elegance. When he retired in 1977, Brazil's ambassador to the UN said that he had done more for goodwill and friendship towards his country, than all the ambassadors ever appointed.

Right: A legendary striker, Pelé had remarkable ball control skills, honed by hours of practice.

Below: Pelé played his last game for Brazil in July 1971 against Yugoslavia.

Edith Piaf

Born Edith Giovanna Gassion
December 19, 1915
Paris, France

Died October 11, 1963
Grasse, France

One of France's most loved singers, Edith Piaf – with her husky, melancholy voice and songs of nostalgia and despair – seemed to reflect her melodramatic life and waif-like appearance in her singing.

The only child of a café singer and a street acrobat, the young Edith was allegedly born on a pavement (though her birth certificate gives a hospital address). She spent part of her childhood in the brothel run by her paternal grandmother. As a teenager, she toured with her father's acrobatic act and supported herself by singing in the streets, although much of this period of her life is obscure.

In 1935, the 19-year-old Piaf was discovered by promoter Louis Leplée, who found her nightclub work and dubbed her *La Môme Piaf*, slang for little sparrow – she was only 4 ft 9 in (1.5 m). Leplée was murdered a year later and Piaf was, at first, regarded as a suspect. Her relationship with lyricist and nightclub manager, Raymond Asso, brought a degree of security; Asso wrote songs inspired by her life and may, or may not have fathered a child with her. By 1939, Piaf was well established on the Parisian nightclub circuit and beginning to make recordings and radio appearances.

Asso was called up at the start of World War II and Piaf seems to have taken charge of her career at this time. She began to write her own lyrics and became one of a circle of noted French artists and entertainers, including Jean Cocteau and Maurice Chevalier, who survived the German occupation as best they could. In 1944, she discovered Yves Montand, who for a time was her lover, as well as part of her act.

In the later 1940s and 1950s, Piaf's fame spread beyond France and she began to tour globally, making her US debut in 1947, but the dramas in her personal life continued. In 1949 her married lover, the middleweight world boxing champion, Marcel Cerdan (and according to some the love of her life), died in a plane crash. In 1951, she was seriously injured in a car accident and became a prey to both morphine and alcohol addiction. Two marriages followed, and she died of liver cancer, aged only 47. Her funeral procession to the Père Lachaise cemetery in Paris drew hundreds of thousands onto the streets of the French capital.

Piaf's performing style was quintessentially French: she sang almost wholly in French, often in Parisian slang, in a loud, rather metallic voice, that was full of character, rather than lovely. Most of the songs were in the classic 'ballad' style – songs of love and loss, of working life, of people and trains leaving, of hopes dashed and the pain of abandonment. Among her most famous numbers are *Non, Je Ne Regrette Rien*, *Les Trois Cloches*, *Vagabond* and *La Vie en Rose*, which was also the title of the award-winning film about her life, released in 2007.

Left: 'For me, singing is a way of escaping,' said Piaf. 'It's another world. I'm no longer on earth.'

Below: In 1952, Piaf married fellow singer, Jacques Pills (centre), who tried to save her from drug addiction.

Pablo Picasso

Born Pablo Diego José Francisco de Paula Juan Nepomuceno María de los Remedios Cipriano de la Santísima Trinidad Ruiz y Picasso
October 25, 1881
Malaga, Spain

Died April 8, 1973
Mougins, France

Innovative, imaginative and technically brilliant, Picasso was arguably the most famous and versatile artist of the 20th century. Always inventive and ahead of his time, he cast a long shadow over later artists and his influence on the world of art was incalculable and enduring.

Picasso was born in Malaga, southern Spain and showed exceptional artistic skill at an early age. He settled in Paris in 1904, where he moved in avant-garde artistic circles, meeting Henri Matisse and selling much of his work to the American writer and collector, Gertrude Stein. Picasso's work in this era had a melancholy quality, often expressed in blue hues, which is why it is known as his Blue Period, best characterized by *La Vie* (1903). His Rose Period from 1905 was less austere and was dominated by clowns, acrobats and harlequins as subject matter.

Les Demoiselles d'Avignon (1907) was his first revolutionary work, marking a real departure from the traditions of European painting. With angular female forms on a fragmented geometric background, it heralded the beginning of Cubism and what would become Picasso's signature style for the next 30 years. Cubism, which Picasso developed with fellow artist Georges Braque, broke objects down into their component shapes and this, in turn, influenced the emergence of Surrealism in the 1920s.

From 1925, Picasso's work became more emotive and expressive, culminating in his vast and most famous painting, *Guernica* (1937) – his expression of horror at the destruction of the Basque town during the Spanish Civil War. *The Charnel House* (1945) echoed this theme with its fragmentary limbs depicted in stark black and grey. 'Painting is not done to decorate apartments,' he said, 'it is an instrument of war against brutality and darkness.'

After World War II, when he had remained in Paris during the German occupation, Picasso's output diversified, as he produced pottery, sculpture and graphic art, as well as paintings. His painting style altered, as he revisited the work of old masters, notably Velásquez, Goya and Poussin.

Picasso's sculpture was less widely known until after his death. He was the first artist to make use of everyday objects – *objets trouvés* – for his sculpture, perhaps the most celebrated being *Head of Bull, Metamorphosis* (1943), made from a bicycle saddle, with handlebars as the horns. His civic sculptures, such as the Chicago Picasso, were often received with bewilderment and protest, but never failed to make an impact on the viewer.

Picasso spent most of his later years in the south of France, where he died at the age of 91. He was prolific throughout his life and his paintings are still considered among the most valuable in the world, regularly setting records at auction.

Right: The artist in his southern France studio, 1950. On the easel is *Paloma and Claude, Children of Picasso.*

Below: Picasso browses a monograph of his finest works published in 1961, to celebrate his 80th birthday.

Pink Floyd

Founded 1965
Disbanded 1996

Members Syd Barrett 1946–2006
David Gilmour 1946–Present
Nick Mason 1944– Present
Roger Waters 1943– Present
Richard Wright 1943–2008

Progressive rock band Pink Floyd were one of the great innovative acts of the 1970s, with a unique sound and strikingly lavish stage shows. Hugely influential, they sold over 200 million albums worldwide.

Founded by students Syd Barrett, Nick Mason and Roger Waters in 1965, Pink Floyd began playing psychedelic music on the London underground scene in the late 1960s, achieving two well-received hits, with the release of the quirky *Arnold Layne* and *See Emily Play* in 1967. Their first album, *The Piper at the Gates of Dawn*, reached No. 6 in the UK chart in 1967 and was a critical and commercial success.

With the eccentric Syd Barrett as their exuberant front man, Pink Floyd were delighted with their initial success. However, it soon became clear that Barrett was more than just eccentric and was suffering either from drug addiction, or more serious mental problems. He was replaced, as lead guitarist by David Gilmour in 1968.

The band released five albums and film soundtracks between 1969 and 1973, among them *Ummagumma* and *Atom Heart Mother*, as they experimented with different sounds and recording processes. But it was *Dark Side of the Moon* (1973) that transformed their moderate success into global recognition and acclaim. The bleak themes of rejection and doom-mongering were subsumed by the unforgettable music and the album remained in the Billboard charts in the US for over a decade. At their best grandiose, thought-provoking and masterful, Pink Floyd combined biting and philosophical lyrics with well-produced orchestral, acoustic and synthesized music.

Pink Floyd became rich and building on the successful formula of Waters' lyrics, backed up by Gilmour's guitar, they released *Wish You Were Here* in 1975, which was dedicated to Syd Barrett. *Animals* (1977), with its surreal album cover of a huge inflatable pig floating above the derelict Battersea Power Station in London, was equally bitter and offered more than a passing nod to George Orwell's novel, *Animal Farm*.

The 1979 album and rock opera *The Wall* was the high point of Pink Floyd's success. Waters' theme of personal isolation won him new young fans with *Another Brick in the Wall*, which begins with the famous words 'We don't need no education ...'. *The Wall* was Pink Floyd's only No. 1 album in the US and earned an even greater accolade in being banned by the BBC.

Relations between the band members became strained in the early 1980s and their last album, *The Final Cut* (1983), made without Richard Wright, was a personal critique by Waters of the UK's postwar legacy. Afterwards, each member pursued a solo career, although in 1987, Mason and Gilmour re-formed, against Waters' wishes, releasing *A Momentary Lapse of Reason*. In 2005, casting their bitterness aside, all four band members played together at the Live 8 concert.

Left: Nick Mason, Richard Wright and Ian Gilmour, who re-formed Pink Floyd in the late 1980s without Roger Waters.

Below: Pink Floyd playing at the Oakland Coliseum in 1977.

Harry Potter

First published June 30, 1997

Harry Potter, the boy wizard, is the fictional creation of the British author, J.K. Rowling and the hero of seven best-selling novels, written between 1997 and 2007.

At the start of the first novel, young, orphaned Harry Potter discovers, on his 11th birthday that he is a wizard. His departure for the wizards' boarding school, Hogwarts, enables him to escape from a miserable life with his spiteful aunt and uncle and Harry discovers a whole new world – one in which he is something of a celebrity. For the first time in his life, he is happy and totally at home. Along with his friends, Ron and Hermione and guided by the powerfully avuncular headmaster, Dumbledore, Harry embarks on a series of adventures battling dragons, spells and the dark evil of Lord Voldemort, the wizard who murdered his parents.

Part of the charm of the world of Harry Potter is the easy mixing of the 'muggle' (ordinary human) and wizarding worlds, where a real London railway station can have a platform invisible to muggles and where wizards can travel by train, or the more traditional magical broomstick. Readers can easily imagine that they, too, might have wizarding blood, as yet undetected and the twisting and adventurous plots further increase their emotional investment in the stories. The books follow classic themes of a young, orphaned and ill-treated hero, who triumphs over every adversity to avenge his parents' death and to smite evil in the process. Though aimed at children, they have an appeal for young and old alike.

The rags to riches story of J.K. Rowling is well known – an impecunious single mother, she penned the first of her fantasy novels in cafés, only to have it rejected by 12 publishers. Undeterred, she planned and created a rich and intricate world of wizards, witches and fantastical beasts, existing alongside, but largely invisible, to ordinary human society.

Finally, in 1997, Bloomsbury, then a small British publisher, printed a short print run of 1,000 copies of *Harry Potter and the Philosopher's Stone*. It was instantly popular and was followed, in 1998 and 1999, by the second and third installments. In the early years of the new century, the annual appearance of the latest Harry Potter was an international publishing event, with fans waiting in line for the midnight release of the books. The sixth novel, *Harry Potter and the Half-Blood Prince*, published in 2005, sold 9 million copies in the first 24 hours. The books have been made into blockbusting films by Warner Brothers, which are among the highest grossing movies of all time.

The international success of Rowling's creation is credited with encouraging a generation of children to read more, with adding a new classic character to the pantheon of English literature and helping to revitalize a flagging sector of the publishing industry.

Below: Author J. K. Rowling on board the Hogwarts Express to publicize *Harry Potter and the Goblet of Fire*, 2000.

Right: Harry Potter actor, Daniel Radcliffe, arriving at the premiere of *Harry Potter and the Order of the Phoenix*, held at Grauman's Chinese Theater in Hollywood.

Elvis Presley

Born Elvis Aaron Presley
January 8, 1935
Tupelo, Mississippi, USA

Died August 16, 1977
Memphis, Tennessee, USA

Elvis Presley was the first and greatest rock 'n' roll singer, whose impact on the world of popular music earned him the nickname, the 'King of Rock 'n' Roll.'

When Elvis first burst on to the scene in 1954, popular music was all about the suave crooning of mature singers, such as Frank Sinatra and Dean Martin.
The impact of the snarling, energetic and captivating boy from the Deep South was electrifying. He sang like no one before him, injecting his songs with a new beat-driven sound, based on a combination of country music, gospel and black R&B. Young and good-looking, Elvis personified a heady and revolutionary image, that terrified the older generation and thrilled his contemporaries.

Presley came from a poor background and never had any formal musical training. He signed with Sun Records in 1954, after stepping inside to make a recording for his mother. His first single, *That's All Right*, took the local radio stations by storm and Elvis's career took off. Just 18 months later he had his first No. 1 hit, with *Heartbreak Hotel*. By September 1956, he was a national star, appearing on the *Ed Sullivan Show* to some 60 million viewers. In many of his TV appearances, he was filmed only from the waist up, so that audiences could not be shocked by the famous gyrating pelvis.

In November 1956, Elvis's first movie, *Love Me Tender*, was released and he had secured his place as the first symbol of teenage culture in the USA. By the time he was drafted into the army in March 1958, Elvis had released four movies and achieved ten No. 1 singles and four albums. He had purchased Graceland, the large mansion in Memphis that became

his retreat and his every public move was accompanied by a horde of screaming girls. He was concerned that two years away from the limelight on military service in Germany would kill his career, but canny record executives had hoarded material to release while he was away. When he was discharged in 1960, the fans who mobbed his train, told him that he had certainly not been forgotten.

During the 1960s, Elvis's manager, Colonel Tom Parker, lined up a punishing schedule of movies, with a series of 27 formulaic films that almost destroyed his career. But the 1968 'Comeback Special' put a leather-clad Elvis back on stage, doing what he did best and marked the beginning of a new era of live performances in the USA.

The collapse of his marriage in 1971 prompted an addiction to prescription drugs, which eventually killed him on August 16, 1977, at the age of 42. But Elvis' versatile voice and natural charisma ensured that his fans remained loyal beyond his untimely death. He remains a peerless icon of the musical world.

Left: Elvis is the best-selling solo artist in the history of popular music – over 50 years after his career began, no one has bettered his record.

Below: Famous for his energetic live performances, Elvis said, 'If I stand still when I'm singin' I'm a dead man.'

The Rolling Stones

The Stones are one of the few groups from the vibrant 1960s, who are still going strong – despite changes in line-up – and performing as raunchily and successfully as ever, after nearly 50 years.

Founder members and boyhood friends Mick Jagger and Keith Richards got together in 1960 to share a taste for American R&B and to form their first band.

They soon met guitarist, Brian Jones and on July 12, 1962, played their first gig as the Rolling Stones, featuring Jagger, Richards and Jones, with bassist Dick Taylor, keyboardist Ian Stewart and Tony Chapman on drums. Bill Wyman soon replaced Taylor and in January 1963 drummer Charlie Watts was persuaded to give up his job in advertising to join the line-up.

The band's successful season in spring 1963, at a west London club attracted ex-Beatles publicist Andrew Loog Oldham, on the lookout for a competitor to The Beatles' clean-cut image. Their first singles were cover versions and they finally had a UK No. 1 with *It's All Over Now* in June 1964. What established the band, however, was their emphasis on black American blues and R&B – much influenced by the music of Chuck Berry and Muddy Waters – in contrast to the Mersey Sound of The Beatles. They were also renowned for their sensational, drug-fueled live performances, which brought them shocked press coverage. Their US tour, in June 1964, was a huge success, with riots in Chicago; their version of the blues standard *Little Red Rooster*, a UK No. 1, was banned in the US for its 'objectionable' lyrics.

In the mid-1960s, Oldham encouraged Jagger and Richards to begin writing their own numbers, which led to a string of pioneering, sophisticated and ironic singles – *The Last Time*, *(I Can't Get No) Satisfaction*, *Get Off My Cloud*, *19th Nervous Breakdown* and *Mother's Little Helper*. In January 1967, the Stones caused a sensation when they performed *Let's Spend the Night Together* on the *Ed Sullivan Show* – with Jagger mumbling

the lines after threats of censorship. The bad-boy image was reinforced later that year, by the arrest in the UK of Jagger, Richards and Jones on drugs possession charges and the death of Brian Jones from a drug overdose, in summer 1969.

In the 1970s, the band seemed, for a while, to lose direction, but their three-yearly US tours were all sell-outs. In 1976, Ronnie Wood became Jones's replacement. Jagger and Richards fell out in the 1980s and there was a recording lull, while bassist Bill Wyman quit in 1992. But although the Stones' album sales generally slowed, the band was and continues to be, a sell-out on tour. Their 'Bigger Bang' tour, which ran for two years from 2005, was the highest grossing tour of all time and even took in the 2006 Super Bowl. It was immortalized by film-maker Martin Scorsese *in Shine a Light* (2008).

Founded	1962
Founder members:	Mick Jagger, Keith Richards, Brian Jones, Dick Taylor, Ian Stewart, Tony Chapman
Current members:	Mick Jagger, Keith Richards, Ronnie Wood, Charlie Watts

Left: The Stones in their heyday, New York, 1964. From left, Jagger, Jones, Wyman, Richards and Watts.

Below: The Stones during the 2006 Superbowl.

Overleaf: Jagger's performances remain as lively as ever.

Diana Ross

Born Diana Ernestine Earle Ross
March 26, 1944
Detroit, Michigan, USA

American singer and actress, Diana Ross, was the most successful female vocalist of the rock era. She played a crucial role in the creation of the 1960s Motown Sound, as lead singer of the female vocal group, the Supremes and went on to launch a hugely successful solo career.

Like many of her contemporaries, Ross learned to sing and harmonize in her local Baptist church choir. She was soon singing with Florence Ballard and Mary Wilson in a girls' vocal group, the Primettes. The time was ripe: Berry Gordy founded the first African-American-owned labels, Tamla Records in 1959 and Motown Records in 1960, in Ross's home town of Detroit. By the time the Primettes auditioned for the label in 1962, Motown was on the way to becoming a major force in the music industry, with its pop-influenced soul sound.

Gordy recognized the group's cross-over potential, signing them up and changing their name to the Supremes. Initially, they worked as a backing group for solo artists, such as Marvin Gaye and Mary Wells. Their first eight singles went nowhere and it was August 1964, before they had the first of five successive No. 1 hits with *Where Did Our Love Go*. The hits that followed, including *Baby Love*, made the group the most successful in the US in the 1960s, and they were only outstripped globally by The Beatles.

From an early stage, Gordy saw Ross, with her alluring stage presence and soaring, well-trained voice, as a potential solo performer and Ross had the ambition to match. Following Ballard's departure in 1967, the group began to be marketed as Diana Ross and the Supremes. Then, in 1969, Ross embarked on her solo career with the album *Diana Ross* and her first hit single *Ain't No Mountain High Enough*. The following year, *I'm Still Waiting* became her first UK No. 1.

A string of television appearances was followed by her acclaimed role in *Lady Sings the Blues* (1972), a biopic of jazz icon Billie Holliday. Ross's casting was initially ridiculed, on the grounds that her persona and singing style were very different from Holliday's. But she immersed herself in the music and won universally favorable reviews and even an Oscar nomination. Several more film roles followed, including *Mahogany* (1975) and the loss-making *The Wiz* (1978).

The 1980s saw a change of record label, with Ross moving to MCA and scoring a hit with *Muscles* (1982), written by her friend and protégé, Michael Jackson. Though sales faltered in the 1980s and 1990s, she continued to make regular television appearances. A planned Supremes tour in 2000 was much criticized for failing to include founder member Mary Wilson and was eventually canceled. The recordings continued, however, with an album of love songs in 2006, *I Love You*. In 2007, Ross's achievements were recognized with a John F. Kennedy Center for the Performing Arts Honors Award.

Left: Diana Ross and the Supremes (left, Florence Ballard, center, Mary Wilson), 1965.

Below: Ross wears a flamboyant headdress during a 2004 concert in Rotterdam, the Netherlands.

Michael Schumacher

German racing driver, Michael Schumacher ('Schumi' or 'Schuey'), has won the Formula One World Championship a record-breaking seven times. He also holds the Formula One records for most race victories, most wins in a season, most career pole positions, most points in a season and most consecutive World Championships – five between 2000 and 2004.

The young Michael showed his racing passion early and was introduced to karting by his parents, winning his first club championship aged only six and swiftly attracting sponsorship from local businessmen. Unable to get a karting license in Germany until he was 14, he obtained one in Luxembourg at the age of 12 and won the German Junior Kart championship in 1982. Leaving school to become a mechanic, he took his first step into single-seat car racing in 1988, winning the German Formula König series. In 1990, he won the German Formula Three championship and was hired by Mercedes to drive sports cars.

He won his first Formula One race for them in 1992, going on to win another 18 races and two World Championships in his next four seasons. His first championship, in 1994, was marred by claims of technical irregularities and a debatable collision, but Schumacher came back strongly in 1995, to take the title with ease, becoming the youngest ever driver to win the championship twice.

Joining Ferrari for the 1996 season, he began promisingly, with three wins in 1996 and five in 1997, while in 1998, he finished second overall. The serious record breaking began in 2000, when Schumacher became Ferrari's first world champion in 21 years. He went on to win the title for four more successive seasons, the last in 2004, by a massive margin, having won 13 out of the season's 18 races. Announcing his retirement at the end of the 2006 season, he finished with yet more records, scoring seven more victories, to bring his career total to 91 (40 more than his nearest rival).

Born January 3, 1969
Hürth-Hermülheim, near
Cologne, Germany

Throughout his career, Schumacher has been noted for his ability to produce fast laps at the crucial moment, to get the maximum out of his car, while understanding its limits and to make the most of difficult wet conditions, earning him the title *Regenmeister* (rain master). He is widely acknowledged to be the world's best ever racing driver.

On his retirement from racing driving, Schumacher became a consultant to Ferrari, lending his expertise for both car and team development. A planned comeback, in 2009, had to be canceled, after a motor bike crash, but he signed a three-year contract with the Mercedes GP Petronas team in 2009 and returned to Formula One racing in the 2010 season.

Schumacher's Formula One debut was impressive – he qualified seventh for the 1991 Belgian Grand Prix at Spa and was immediately signed by Benetton-Ford.

Right: Schumacher celebrates his win in the Belgian Grand Prix, 1995. Statistically, he is the most successful Formula One driver ever.

Below: Driving for the Ferrari team during the 1997 Spanish Grand Prix.

Arnold Schwarzenegger

Former bodybuilder, Arnold Schwarzenegger, has made a long journey from an Austrian village, first to Hollywood acting glory and then to political power. He is currently serving a second term as the 38th governor of the state of California.

Beginning his bodybuilding career in his early teens, Schwarzenegger won the Junior Mr Europe title in 1965. The following year, he made his first plane trip to take part in the Mr Universe contest in London. Staying on to train with one of the judges, he became the youngest person ever to win the title in 1967.

Schwarzenegger was determined from an early age to get to the US, the land of opportunity. He moved to California in 1968, despite his still basic English and trained at Gold's Gym in Santa Monica. In 1970, he won the Mr Olympia title, the highest accolade in international professional bodybuilding and went on to win it again for five consecutive years, before announcing his retirement in 1975.

Meanwhile he had been working hard to break into films, ignoring discouraging feedback about his unusual appearance and heavy accent. He was Hercules in the dire *Hercules in New York* (1969), where his voice was dubbed to make him comprehensible and then played a deaf-mute in Altman's *The Long Goodbye* (1973), before taking a more substantial role with Jeff Bridges in *Stay Hungry* (1976). The documentary *Pumping Iron* (1976), about the 1975 Mr Olympia competition, first brought Arnie to public attention. But his major breakthrough came with the violent and successful *Conan the Barbarian* (1982), which met

a huge demand for live action movies in the 1980s and led to a host of similar roles. Movies such as *Twins* (1988), with Danny de Vito, demonstrated that Schwarzenegger was not a one-trick wonder and could really act.

Superstardom was assured by what will undoubtedly remain Schwarzenegger's signature part, as the titular character in *The Terminator*, James Cameron's 1984 sci-fi epic and its two sequels. He brought an element of self-deprecating humor and even pathos to what was otherwise an all-action role. *Terminator 2: Judgment Day* was the highest grossing film of 1991 and Schwarzenegger was named International Star of the Decade in 1993.

Schwarzenegger married into American political aristocracy in 1986, when he wed television journalist Maria Shriver, daughter of John F. Kennedy's sister, Eunice. He himself has long been a Republican supporter and accompanied Ronald Reagan's Vice-President, George

Born	Arnold Alois Schwarzenegger July 30, 1947 Thal, Graz, Austria

Bush, on the presidential campaign in 1988. In 2003, he announced his intention to run for the governorship of California and defeated a crowded field of candidates; he was reelected by a substantial majority in 2006. The astute and adaptable Schwarzenegger has proved a relatively moderate and popular governor, making a commitment to tackle global warming and signing into law in 2007, the state's first cap on greenhouse emissions.

Left: Arnie in his most celebrated role, *The Terminator*, 1984.

Below: Elected governor of California in 2003, Schwarzenegger is sometimes nicknamed 'the Governator' in tribute to his most famous role.

The Simpsons

Matt Groening's animated show *The Simpsons* – starring a crazy, but lovable yellow-skinned family – has become the longest-running sitcom in television history. It gave a satirical edge to primetime television in the early 1990s and was a major factor in establishing newcomer, Fox, as a legitimate broadcasting television network.

The series was conceived when cartoonist Groening was invited to pitch ideas for animation shorts to producer James L. Brooks for *The Tracey Ullman Show*. Initially, Brooks wanted him to adapt the characters from his *Life in Hell* cartoon, but Groening was reluctant to jeopardize his ownership rights and instead came up with the idea of a dysfunctional family. The characters first appeared on *The Tracey Ullman Show* on April 19, 1987. Groening submitted basic sketches to the animators, assuming they would be tidied up, but the animators simply retraced his drawings. It was

Created April, 1987

George Peluse, the colorist, who decided to make the characters yellow.

When Brooks negotiated a contract with Fox for a half-hour series called *The Simpsons*, he stipulated the inclusion of a clause preventing Fox from interfering with content. Groening's stated intention was to offer an alternative to 'mainstream trash.' The show is notable not only for its wide-ranging cultural references – which typically include Susan Sontag, Ayn Rand and *The Bridges of Madison County* in a single episode – but also for its raw parodying of the hypocrisies and contradictions found within society. So, dimwit patriarch, Homer, tells bright daughter, Lisa, that it is all right to steal 'from people you don't like' and the Reverend Lovejoy lies to win an argument. Behind them all looms the nuclear power plant, where the lazy and careless Homer works as a safety inspector.

The series premiered on December 17, 1989 and was the first Fox program to

gain a place in a season's Top 30 shows. In most episodes of the first three series, Bart – the delinquent oldest Simpson child – was the lead character. The series has sparked a huge amount of merchandizing: Bart T-shirts have sold millions, helped rather than hindered by the banning in some American schools of T-shirts with slogans, such as 'Underachiever (and proud of it!).'

Early critical reception was ecstatic and the show spawned a whole series of copycat animations, such as the raucous *South Park*. The Simpsons has won numerous honors and awards: in 1998, *Time* magazine named it the 20th century's best television series, while in 2008, it was first on *Entertainment Weekly*'s list of Top 100 shows of the past 25 years. It has notched up a total of 25 Primetime Emmy Awards.

Latterly, there have been some suggestions that it is running out of steam – a charge vigorously denied by Groening. Certainly the spin-offs continue: *The Simpsons Movie* (2007) was both critically and financially a winner. The show's 20th anniversary season in 2009–10 was celebrated by Morgan Spurlock's documentary, *The Simpsons 20th Anniversary Special! In 3–D! On Ice!*, which was shown alongside the 450th episode to celebrate 'the cultural phenomenon of *The Simpsons*.'

Above: Cartoonist and Simpsons' creator Matt Groening poses with the world's favorite yellow family, 1990.

Left: Homer's famous exasperated 'D'oh' is now so well-known that it is listed in the *Oxford English Dictionary*.

Frank Sinatra

Born Francis Albert Sinatra
December 12, 1915
Hoboken, New Jersey,
USA

Died May 14, 1998
Los Angeles, California,
USA

The classic rags-to-riches story of Frank Sinatra, superstar singer and Oscar-winning actor, encapsulates all that is most appealing about 20th-century America. His many nicknames – 'Ol' Blue Eyes', 'The Chairman of the Board' and simply 'The Voice', to name just a few – give some idea of the adulation and respect he commanded.

The only child of Italian immigrants, Sinatra decided early on that he wanted to be a singer. His career began in the big-band 'swing' era: he signed with the Tommy Dorsey Orchestra in 1940, when he first attracted the adulation of teenage fans, the so-called bobbysoxers.

Launching a solo career in 1942, he began a four-week slot on Benny Goodman's post-Christmas show at the New York Paramount on December 30 – and a legend was born. *Variety* hailed him as the 'hottest thing in show-biz' and his live appearances continued to charm audiences worldwide to the end of his career. A contract with Columbia and a series of concerts with four of American's leading orchestras followed in 1943. With his frail and vulnerable image (he was turned down for war service on health grounds), naturally tuneful voice and well-honed technique, he brought passion and feeling back to singing.

Films soon beckoned and in 1945, Sinatra made *Anchors Aweigh* with Gene Kelly, which led to a five-year contract with MGM. The late 1940s saw a slide in his recording career, problems at MGM and a tempestuous on-off relationship with Ava Gardner, that ended his first marriage. But the classic war movie *From Here to Eternity*

(1953), Sinatra's first non-singing role, finally proved that he was an actor as well as a crooner: it won him an Oscar for Best Supporting Actor and relaunched his film career. A string of successful roles followed – a psychopathic assassin in *Suddenly* (1954), the feckless Nathan Detroit in *Guys and Dolls* (1955) with Marlon Brando, a reformed junkie in *The Man with the Golden Arm* (1955) and a hopeful journalist in *High Society* (1956), with Grace Kelly and Bing Crosby.

From the late 1950s, Sinatra launched into the album market and focused on a more adult audience, now that rock was taking over the hit parade. *Songs for Swingin' Lovers!* (1956), a subtle big band album, including all-time favorites such as *I've Got You Under My Skin* and *You Make Me Feel So Young*, was an early high point. He also turned successful businessman, buying his way into legalized gambling in Nevada and establishing his own hugely successful record label, Reprise, in 1960. A brief retirement (1971–3) ended with another flow of recordings and sell-out live appearances. Frank Sinatra's 75th birthday tour in 1990 was a critical triumph and in 1995, to mark his 80th birthday, the Empire State Building glowed blue.

Right: Ol' Blue Eyes in 1954 at the height of his fame.

Below: Sinatra retired in 1971, but returned to recording just two years later and by the early 1980s, had revived his popularity.

The Spice Girls

Founded 1994

Members:
Victoria Beckham (*née* Adams)
Melanie Brown
Emma Bunton
Melanie Chisholm
Geri Halliwell

A British girl band and global and cultural phenomenon, the Spice Girls were the first major 1990s pop group to have their roots not in rock music, but in dance and modeling. They pioneered the commercial breakthrough of teen pop and personified the celebrity-obsessed 'Cool Britannia' of the 1990s.

The band began with an advertisement. Heart Management saw the potential for a girl band to compete with boy bands such as Take That and placed an ad in *The Stage* trade magazine in February 1994. The resulting five-girl group, initially called Touch, went through various personnel changes, as they began working together, with only Victoria Adams, Melanie Brown and Geri Halliwell surviving from the first intake. Melanie Chisholm and Emma Bunton arrived later in the year.

The group soon bonded and unhappy with Heart's failure to give them a contract, began writing their own songs and touring their demos round management agencies. They finally signed a management contract with Simon Fuller of 19 Entertainment in March 1995 and a recording deal with Virgin Records in September. Their first single, *Wannabe*, was released in the summer of 1996 in the UK and became the first debut single by an all-girl band to go straight into the charts at No. 1, where it stayed for seven weeks.

Brilliantly marketed from the outset, the Spice Girls appeared as individual personalities: Posh Spice (Adams), Scary Spice (Brown), Sexy Spice (Halliwell), Sporty Spice (Chisholm) and Baby Spice (Bunton) all immediately established themselves in the British celebrity press and have remained there ever since, with varying degrees of success. They made their mark with an accessible mix of hip-hop and pop balladry, directly targeted at a teen market, while preaching an appealing would-be feminist 'Girl Power.'

The release of *Wannabe* in the US in January 1997 was followed by their debut album *Spice*, which proved a hit on both sides of the Atlantic. Sales in the UK made the Spice Girls the fastest selling British act since The Beatles, while in the US, *Spice* was the biggest selling album of 1997. Their promotional videos became collectables in their own right and the next step, *Spice World the Movie* (1997), cemented the Spice Girls' fame. The first two single releases from the movie, *Spice Up Your Life* and *Too Much*, went straight into the UK charts at No. 1, giving the band six consecutive No. 1 hits.

However, cracks were showing: in late 1997, the band decided to part with Fuller and manage their own affairs, in 1998, Geri announced her departure and in 2001, the remaining four performers decided to concentrate on their solo careers. They did not disband the group, though and retained their mystique into the 21st century. A reunion tour of all five Spice Girls in 2007–8 was an immediate sell-out, prompting frequent rumors of further reunions.

Left: The Spice Girls perform at the 12th Annual Victoria's Secret Fashion Show, Kodak Theatre, Hollywood, California, November 15, 2007.

Steven Spielberg

Born Steven Allan Spielberg
December 18, 1946
Cincinnati, Ohio, USA

American film-maker and director Steven Spielberg has, in a 50-year career, made some of the top grossing and most culturally significant movies of all time. They range from the primeval terror of *Jaws*, through live action delights such as *Raiders of the Lost Ark*, to serious period pieces, including *Schindler's List* and *Saving Private Ryan*.

Spielberg began filming early, making his first short aged just ten and completing a full-length sci-fi feature called *Firelight* by his mid-teens. He worked first in television, directing the taut *Duel* (1971), about a vengeful truck-driver who tries to force a small car off the road; the TV film was later expanded for movie release. His breakthrough came with *Jaws* (1975), in which a great white shark terrorizes a coastal community. The filming itself was a near-run thing – the shoot was difficult and overran and Spielberg was nearly replaced. But his masterly management of the growing suspense and the clever action sequences made it a smash hit, beginning a trend for summer blockbusters that both kids and parents could enjoy. He followed this up with the mystical sci-fi thriller *Close Encounters of the Third Kind* (1977), the swashbuckling action movie *Raiders of the Lost Ark* (1981) and the emotive and enormously successful *ET* (1982).

Spielberg was box office heaven, but the critics were unconvinced – Oscar-nominated as Best Director for these three films, he was overlooked each time. His next work included two heavyweight literary adaptations, *The Color Purple* (1985), based on Alice Walker's novel of self-discovery, and *Empire of the Sun* (1987), based on J.G. Ballard's tale of childhood in a Japanese prisoner-of-war camp.

But he and his public still loved a suspense story and *Jurassic Park* (1993), with its brilliantly convincing computer-generated monsters, outstripped even ET, as the biggest grossing film ever.

Finally Spielberg embarked on a project he had been planning for years – his adaptation of Thomas Keneally's novel about Oskar Schindler, the industrialist who risked his life and fortune to save over 1,000 Jews during World War II. Shot in somber black and white, with Liam Neeson magisterial in the lead role, *Schindler's List* (1993) garnered seven Oscars, including, at last, Best Picture and Best Director.

After a break from directing during which he co-founded the major studio Dreamworks, Spielberg returned to directing with *Saving Private Ryan* (1998), set during the invasion of Normandy in June 1944. The movie is most notable for its sustained opening D-Day landing sequence, which was hailed as one of the most stunning battle scenes ever filmed.

More recent successes have included the visually inventive and futuristic *Minority Report* (2002), the enjoyable thriller *Catch Me If You Can* (2002), an adaptation of H.G. Wells's *The War of the Worlds* (2005) and yet another action movie, *Indiana Jones and the Kingdom of the Crystal Skull* (2008). In 2001, Spielberg was awarded a British honorary knighthood for services to film.

Right: Spielberg is a prolific and extremely successful film-maker, whose movies encompass several genres. A master of fast-action thrillers – more than just the standard Hollywood blockbuster – he has also produced some of the most thought-provoking movies of recent years.

Born Bruce Frederick Joseph
Springsteen
September 23, 1949
Long Branch, New Jersey,
USA

Bruce Springsteen

American rock singer and guitarist, Bruce Springsteen – nicknamed 'The Boss' – was one of the most important musicians to emerge in the 1970s. An early and passionate believer in the redemptive power of rock music, he put the dramas and emotions of everyday life into his songs and successfully combined celebrity status with his populist style. By the 1980s, he was established as one of the world's most popular white rock stars.

Springsteen bought his first guitar aged 13 and played with a number of bands in his teens, already writing his own numbers. In May 1972 he signed a management contract with Laurel Canyon Productions, who swiftly got him a ten-album recording deal with Columbia. Within a month, Springsteen had completed *Greetings from Asbury Park, N.J.* Neither this, nor his follow-up album, *The Wild, the Innocent and the E Street Shuffle*, attracted more than cult attention and Springsteen decided to concentrate on live performance, developing what became the E Street Band.

A rave review in spring 1974 and his breakthrough third album *Born to Run*, considered by many to be his finest and one of the best rock and roll albums of all time, combined to establish Springsteen as a genuinely new sound and launch him towards commercial success. In the same week, in October 1974, he appeared on the covers of both *Time* and *Newsweek*.

Unable to record for 18 months, during a legal dispute with his management company, Springsteen instead focused on hugely successful live shows and on song-writing. Patti Smith, the Hollies and Manfred Mann all had hits in the 1970s with Springsteen numbers. His powerful comeback album, *Darkness on the Edge of Town* (1978), featured an emotional exploration of working-class hopes and problems.

However, it was not until the consciously popularizing *Born in the U.S.A.* (1984), that Springsteen finally realized his megastar potential. The album produced a string of singles, that included *Dancing in the Dark*, *Born in the U.S.A.*, *Glory Days* and *My Hometown* and was packaged with a US flag on the cover. President Reagan's attempt to claim Springsteen's vision as his own was rejected by its originator, who was always a supporter of labor, the environment and civil rights. In 1988, he headlined the Amnesty International 'Human Rights Now!' tour, although overall, the late 1980s and 1990s were a less productive time for him.

In 1999, Springsteen reunited with the E Street Band, after more than a decade, for a record-setting US tour. The 21st century has seen a return to mainstream success and to clear political engagement, with his endorsement of Democratic presidential candidates John Kerry in 2004 and Barack Obama in 2008. The accessible album *Magic* proved a popular hit in 2007 and in December 2009, Springsteen was awarded a Kennedy Center Honor for his contribution to American culture.

Left and right: The archetypal blue-collar musical hero, Springsteen has maintained a consistent image throughout his long career, although each successive album has something new for his fans.

Howard Stern

Born Howard Allan Stern
January 12, 1954
Queens, New York City,
USA

American 'shock jock', Howard Stern, the highest paid radio personality in the US, came to national prominence in the 1990s, with his explicit and provocative morning radio show.

A bright child and an early radio fan, Stern was attracted to Boston University in 1972, because of its reputation in broadcast communications and graduated magna cum laude in 1976. His early experience was at rock radio stations in New York, Hartford and Detroit, followed by the station DC-101 in Washington DC, where he more than tripled his audience in little over a year, with his mix of music and playful phone calls. In 1982, he signed a five-year deal with NBC for the afternoon program on their flagship WNBC station in New York City. Already, some of Stern's comic material had upset listeners, however and NBC monitored his show intensely. At first, Stern played ball, but gradually he introduced slots, such as 'Sexual Innuendo Wednesday' and 'Mystery Whiz' and in 1985, he was fired.

It was at New York City's WXRK station, better known as K-ROCK, that Stern really got going. Establishing his own on-air team and provocatively confronting touchy subjects that others preferred to avoid – like race, sex and death – he soon earned top ratings on his morning program, where he stayed for nearly 20 years. In 1986, he syndicated his show, allowing him to break into other US markets – first Philadelphia and Washington DC and ultimately, Los Angeles, New Orleans, Boston and Dallas. In 1992, he was the first to top New York and Los Angeles ratings simultaneously, by 1993, he was claiming 3 million daily listeners and by 1995, he was reportedly earning $8 million a year.

His autobiography, characteristically called *Private Parts*, hit the bestseller list in 1993 and stayed there for a month, proving the fastest selling title in its publisher's history.

The outrageousness continued, with Stern causing deep offence, by his would-be humorous comments on the murder of the Mexican American singer Selena in 1995 and on the Columbine High School shootings in 1999. By 2004 his employers had been fined some $2.5 million in total by the Federal Communications Commission, for breaches of the broadcasting code and he was dropped by the US media giant Clear Channel.

It was at this point that Stern changed the face of American radio by quitting the public airwaves. Instead, he signed a five-year $500 million contract with the unregulated subscription satellite network, Sirius, saying 'I left because I couldn't stand the censorship'. His move helped catapult satellite radio to public awareness. When he announced his move, Sirius had 650,000 listeners. In 2005, it added 2.2 million new subscribers and by the end of 2008, could boast more than 19 million.

Right and below: In 2006, Stern began to broadcast for the Sirius satellite radio service, an unregulated radio station, where his particular brand of trenchant commentary is uncensored.

Barbra Streisand

Born Barbara Joan Streisand
April 24, 1942
Brooklyn, New York, USA

Singer, actress and director, Barbra Streisand, is a legend in the entertainment world. Her vocal and acting talents have earned her more accolades and awards than most of her contemporaries and with 141 million album sales worldwide, she is the best-selling female artist of all time.

Having won a talent competition in a New York City nightclub, Streisand became a cabaret singer while still in her teens, although her ambitions were originally to act. She received little encouragement from her family, but took acting lessons and somehow overcame chronic stage fright, to wow her audiences. She also dropped the middle 'a' from her first name, to make it stand out.

In 1962, she made her Broadway debut in the musical *I Can Get It for You Wholesale*, for which – unusually for a newcomer – she won a Tony nomination. A recording contract with Columbia Records was swift to follow and in 1963, her first album (the first of 35 studio recordings), *The Barbra Streisand Album*, earned two Grammy awards. Aged just 21, she was the youngest artist to receive this honor. Her Broadway career continued in 1964, with her role as the comedian Fanny Brice in *Funny Girl*, which she took to London in 1966 and turned into an Oscar-winning performance in the 1968 movie.

Streisand had proven that she was a performer of substance. Her film career continued with the musicals *Hello Dolly* (1969) and *On a Clear Day You Can See Forever* (1970), before diverting into a couple of screwball comedies, notably *What's Up, Doc?* in 1972. She received an Oscar nomination for her engaging performance opposite Robert Redford in *The Way We Were* (1973) and her performance of the film's title track earned Streisand her first No. 1 single in the US. Her second chart hit, *Evergreen*, came from her next movie, *A Star is Born* (1976), for which she also won her second Oscar, this time as composer for Best Original Song.

Towards the end of the 1970s, Streisand had a succession of Top 10 hits, including the collaboration with her high school classmate, Neil Diamond on *You Don't Bring Me Flowers*. In 1980, her most popular album so far, *Guilty*, produced another No. 1 hit, *Woman in Love*.

In 1983, Streisand realized a long-held ambition, when she directed, co-wrote, produced and starred in *Yentl*, which won her Golden Globes for Best Director and Best Comedy/Musical. She repeated the experience as writer, director and star with two more movies, *The Prince of Tides* (1991) and *The Mirror Has Two Faces* (1996). After a long break from live concerts, she returned to singing in public again in 1993 and has since performed in several sell-out concert tours in the USA, Canada and Europe. Her many devoted fans ensure that tickets sell out within hours of their release.

Left and right: The musical *Hello Dolly* (1969) was one of Streisand's earliest hits

Quentin Tarantino

Born Quentin Jerome Tarantino
March 27, 1963
Knoxville, Tennessee, USA

When American film director, Quentin Tarantino, burst on to the international scene in 1992, with his stylized gangster movie *Reservoir Dogs*, he became an overnight sensation. His movies have since been much imitated and are characterized by imaginative, bizarre plot lines, intense bursts of violence and witty dialogue.

Born in Tennessee, Tarantino grew up in California, where his early love of film led him to drop out of school to work in a video store. He worked alongside fellow film buff, Roger Avary, who later became his collaborator, sharing the Oscar for Best Original Screenplay for *Pulp Fiction*.

While dispensing his movie knowledge to customers by day, Tarantino spent his spare time working on the screenplays that would eventually become *True Romance* and *Natural Born Killers*. He also managed to gain a bit part in the sitcom *The Golden Girls* and forged the connections necessary to get his scripts into the hands of influential film producers.

His debut movie *Reservoir Dogs* was a low-budget, independent production, that received little attention in the US, but was immediately popular in Britain, where it won critical praise and sky-high box office receipts. Shown at the Sundance Film Festival, it suddenly caught the critics' attention and the spotlight turned to the director. Vilified for the film's violence and bad language, Tarantino was unapologetic, stating that he wanted to provoke a reaction from his audiences.

Tarantino gained recognition from Hollywood with the release of his second movie, *Pulp Fiction*, in 1994. The film, starring John Travolta and Samuel L. Jackson, was notable for its violence and bad language, diluted by mordant black humor and a complex nonlinear plot. Following this success, *True Romance*, with a screenplay by Tarantino, was released in 1993. A romantic crime film, it was not directed by Tarantino, but once again, audiences were dazzled by its pop culture references, sharp bursts of violence and innovative plot twists.

Tarantino continued to court controversy with *Jackie Brown* (1997), his homage to the 'blaxploitation' movies of the 1970s (which had targeted urban black audiences). Similarly, the two-part action thriller *Kill Bill* (2003 and 2004), his take on martial arts and revenge movies, also polarized the critics. *Inglourious Basterds* (2009) tackled the war movie genre with Tarantino's customary originality and earned eight Academy Award nominations.

Aside from his startlingly creative screenplays, Tarantino specializes in reviving the careers of 'resting' stars – such as John Travolta in *Pulp Fiction*, Pam Grier in *Jackie Brown* and David Carradine in *Kill Bill*. This adds another dimension to his movies, as audiences are astounded and usually delighted to see old stars reappearing on the screen in surprising roles. Rather like Alfred Hitchcock, Tarantino appears in cameo roles in several of his movies, but it is for his ground-breaking work behind the camera that he stands out.

Above: Tarantino at Cannes, 2001.

Right: Quentin Tarantino arrives with actress, Melanie Laurent, at the Golden Globe Awards in Beverly Hills, January 2010.

Elizabeth Taylor

Born   Elizabeth Rosemond
Taylor
February 27, 1932
London, England

Screen legend, Elizabeth Taylor, began her career as a child star in 1941, during the golden age of Hollywood. Her charisma, beauty and talent swiftly propelled her to the pinnacle of Hollywood fame. The winner of two Oscars for Best Actress, she is as well known for her colorful private life, as for her long movie career.

Born in London to American parents, Taylor moved back to the US with her family on the outbreak of World War II. Encouraged by her mother, the young Elizabeth appeared in her first film at the age of nine. But it was her second, *Lassie Come Home* (1943), in which she co-starred with Roddy McDowall, that made her name. Her performance in *National Velvet* (1944) catapulted her to true stardom, as audiences were captivated by her engaging character and luminous beauty. She was also popular with the MGM studio, as a competent and bankable star and was nicknamed 'One-shot Liz', for her ability to shoot a scene in just one take.

Taylor graduated to adult roles with her performance alongside Spencer Tracy in the 1950 romantic comedy *Father of the Bride*. The following year she really proved she could handle a serious dramatic role in *A Place in the Sun*, in which she played a spoiled socialite opposite Montgomery Clift, to great critical acclaim. She was never short of work in the 1950s, but gave her most memorable performances opposite Rock Hudson and James Dean in *Giant* (1956) and with Paul Newman in *Cat on a Hot Tin Roof* (1958). She won her first Oscar for *Butterfield 8* in 1960.

Also, in 1960, she became the highest paid actress in the world, when she was cast in the title role, opposite Richard

Burton, in *Cleopatra* (released in 1963). Art collided with life on the set of the movie, when Taylor, already a veteran of four marriages, began an affair with Burton, whom she would later marry – twice. She played opposite Burton several times during the 1960s, notably in *Who's Afraid of Virginia Woolf?*, when her performance as the bitter, hard-drinking harridan, Martha, earned her a second Best Actress Oscar in 1966.

During the 1970s, Taylor's on-off relationship with Burton garnered rather more interest than her movies, though she made her Broadway debut, in 1982, in Lillian Hellman's *The Little Foxes*. The onset of the AIDS crisis in the early 1980s and the death of her co-star and friend Rock Hudson, prompted Taylor to begin fundraising for AIDS charities and she

has since devoted a great deal of time to humanitarian work.

In recent years, she has given cameo performances, but has been plagued by ill health. Nevertheless, she remains a Hollywood legend – and perhaps the last great star – famous for her eight marriages, her devoted friendship with Michael Jackson, her charitable work and the legacy of her unforgettable screen performances.

Right: Burton and Taylor smoldering in *Cleopatra*.

Below: Taylor in *Suddenly, Last Summer*, 1960.

Overleaf: With Louis Jourdan in *The V.I.P.s*, 1963.

Mother Teresa

Mother Teresa was the most famous nun of the 20th century, internationally renowned for her humanitarian work in the slums of Calcutta. After her death in 1997, she was beatified by Pope John Paul II, as the Blessed Teresa of Calcutta.

Born in Macedonia to an Albanian family, Agnes Bojaxhiu felt a strong religious vocation from an early age and as young as 12, wanted to take up a religious life. Having begun to work as a missionary, with the Irish Sisters of Loreto when she was 18, she traveled to Ireland to learn English, so that she could conduct missionary work in India. She began her novitiate in Darjeeling, near the Himalayan mountains, in 1929.

She took full solemn vows in 1937, assuming the religious name Teresa, after the visionary St. Thérèse of Lisieux, the patron saint of missionaries. Deeply struck by the poverty around her in Calcutta, in 1948 she was given permission to leave her job as a teacher in the city, to work among the poor in the slums. Totally reliant on goodwill, volunteers and charitable donations, Mother Teresa somehow alleviated the suffering of the poor, the desperately ill and the dying. She began an open-air school for slum children and in 1950, received permission from the Vatican to found the organization that would become the Missionaries of Charity, devoted to caring for those whom nobody else was prepared to look after. With only 13 members at its foundation,

Born Agnes Gonxha Bojaxhiu
August 26, 1910
Skopje, Macedonia

Died September 5, 1997
Calcutta, India

the order now has some 4,000 nuns who run orphanages, hospices and charitable institutions around the world.

With great dedication and energy, Mother Teresa battled against her own personal demons to carry out what she saw as God's work, relentlessly striving to provide help for lepers, orphaned children and the terminally ill. From India, the order extended throughout the 1960s and 1970s to South America, the USA, Africa and Europe, gradually attracting more charitable donations. Awarded the Nobel Peace Prize in 1979, Mother Teresa personally intervened in the Lebanon conflict in 1982, rescuing 37 children

trapped by the war. She also traveled to Ethiopia, Chernobyl and Armenia to help victims of disasters, both natural and manmade.

Though Mother Teresa was lauded by many during her lifetime as a living saint, her work was not without criticism from doctors and journalists who questioned her motivation. It is undeniable, however, that she improved the lives of a great many people throughout the developing world.

Mother Teresa was honored internationally and continued to work until six months before her death, despite suffering two

heart attacks and other health problems. When she died at her home in India, she was given a state funeral by the Indian government.

Left: Diminutive, determined and steely, Mother Teresa spoke out on behalf of the poor and oppressed.

Below: Mother Teresa listens to mass celebrated by Pope John Paul II in Ranchi in the state of Bihar during his official visit to India, 1986.

Tina Turner

Born Anna Mae Bullock
November 28, 1939
Nutbush, Tennessee, USA

With her powerful voice, gutsy stage performances and exuberant costumes, Tina Turner is one of the world's great and most enduring rock goddesses. Her career has been something of a rollercoaster and solo success came to her late, but her persistence, charisma and sheer talent have combined to make her a legendary performer.

Born in Nutbush, Tennessee, she met musician Ike Turner, the man who became her first husband, in a nightclub in St. Louis when she was 18 and persuaded him to employ her, as a backing singer for his Kings of Rhythm Band. Ike soon realized that Anna Mae was more than just a backing singer and in 1960, *A Fool in Love*, with 'Little Ann' on lead vocals, became an R&B hit. Exercising the control for which he became notorious, Ike changed her name to Tina and the band became the Ike and Tina Turner Revue, releasing a string of hits in the 1960s, such as *Tra La La La La* and the landmark *River Deep – Mountain High* (1966). The Revue performed dynamic stage sets, with Tina backed by a group of female singers. Their final hit, as the Turners' marriage disintegrated, was in 1973, with *Nutbush City Limits*, written by Tina about her home town.

When she left Ike, Tina gained emotional freedom from his bullying and drug abuse, but she suffered financial problems and struggled to recapture her musical popularity at the end of the 1970s, particularly in the US. She remained extremely popular in Europe, though, where her concerts continued to sell out.

Tina's career turned around in 1984, with the release and forceful promotion of *What's Love Got to Do with It*. Probably her most popular single, it became her only No. 1 in the US and did well in the Top Ten of several European charts. The album *Private Dancer* (1984) yielded several more hits, including the title track and *Better Be Good To Me*, and earned Turner four Grammy awards. She capitalized on her success with a sell-out 'Private Dancer' tour and a role in *Mad Max Beyond Thunderdome* (1985), co-starring with Mel Gibson.

Since then, Tina Turner has never really looked back. She has toured tirelessly, performed with stars, such as Mick Jagger and Eric Clapton and recorded iconic songs, such as *The Best* (1989) and the theme to the James Bond movie, *Goldeneye* (1995).

With her trademark big hair, fantastically toned legs and skimpy skirts, Tina Turner belies her age and continues to belt out energetic performances to sell-out crowds – she has sold more concert tickets than any other solo performer.

Feted at the Kennedy Center Honors in 2005, Turner was praised for her lifetime contribution to American culture as 'simply the best.'

Left: Turner's role in *Mad Max Beyond Thunderdome* helped to re-establish her career.

Below: Tina Turner in concert in London, 1987.

U2

Founded 1976

Members Bono (Paul Hewson)
The Edge (David Evans)
Adam Clayton
Larry Mullen Jr.

Irish rock band U2 are one of the supergroups of the age, a politically conscious band whose music fills stadiums with diehard fans around the globe. They are one of the most commercially successful bands in the world, having sold more than 150 million records and won 22 Grammy awards.

Founded in Dublin in 1976 by 14-year-old drummer Larry Mullen Jr., U2 began life as Feedback and changed their name to The Hype, before settling on U2. Influenced by punk, in 1978, they won a talent show in Limerick, with the prize of recording a demo for CBS Ireland and by 1980, they had released two moderately successful records in Ireland.

With their signing to Island Records and the release of their first album, *Boy*, in 1980, U2's fortunes took off. Bono's earnest lyrics, complemented by the band's dynamic playing, made for formidable live performances and the band consolidated their position as a serious rock band, with the release, in 1983, of the chart-topping album *War*. It included the single *Sunday Bloody Sunday* – a powerful response to the conflict in Northern Ireland – and *New Year's Day*, which reached No. 10 in the UK chart.

The band began a fruitful collaboration in 1984 with producer Brian Eno, who added a new ambient direction and rich orchestral sound to their output on

The Unforgettable Fire (1984). *Pride (In the Name of Love)*, a tribute to Martin Luther King, was their first American hit single. They moved on from this experimentation to embrace the folk and blues roots of American rock on their 1987 album *The Joshua Tree*. The fastest selling album in British chart history, it remained at No. 1 for nine weeks in the US.

Achtung Baby (1991) continued the band's reputation for reinvention, with their music taking on a new feel inspired by dance music. Their live performances on the 'Zoo TV' tour of 1992–3 assumed an extravagant multimedia guise. In their postmodern way, they embraced the excesses of the world of cable TV and satellite news, in order to satirize it and continued to poke fun at commercialism, with their 1997 'Popmart' tour. *All That You Can't Leave Behind* (2000) was classic U2, with an accomplished sound and produced two exceptional singles, *Beautiful Day* and *Stuck in a Moment You Can't Get Out Of*, which supplied two of the album's seven Grammy awards.

Away from the music, U2 have worked to address the world's problems of social injustice and disease and Bono in particular, has concerned himself with global issues of poverty and debt in the developing world. The band continue to tour and make albums, cementing their status as one of the iconic rock acts of recent times.

Left: U2, during the Joshua Tree Tour, 1987. From left to right – Larry Mullen, Jr., The Edge, Bono and Adam Clayton.

Below: Bono performs *In the Name of Love* during the We Are One: Inaugural Celebration at the Lincoln Memorial in Washington to celebrate the presidential inauguration of Barack Obama, 2009.

Andy Warhol

Born Andrew Warhola
August 6, 1928
Pittsburgh, Pennsylvania,
USA

Died February 22, 1987
New York City, USA

Famous for saying that 'In the future everyone will be famous for 15 minutes,' Andy Warhol himself found fame as an innovative artist that lasted much longer. One of the prime movers behind the Pop Art movement of the 1960s, he was an influential and iconoclastic graphic artist and film-maker.

Born in Pittsburgh, Pennsylvania to Slovak immigrants, Warhol studied commercial art at the Carnegie Institute of Technology in Pittsburgh, before moving to New York, in 1949, to work in magazine illustration and advertising. He also began to design album covers in the wake of the rapid expansion of the recording industry at the end of the 1950s and in 1957, his shoe advertisements won an award.

His first solo exhibition, in Los Angeles in November 1962, is regarded as a revolutionary moment in art, when his careful depictions of everyday objects in oils turned art on its head. He embraced the commercialization of society, using mass advertising as the basis for his work and became one of the leading exponents of Pop Art. He drew on iconic American products and people for his inspiration and his first exhibition included the *Marilyn Diptych* (containing 50 images of Marilyn Monroe), *100 Soup Cans* and *100 Coke Bottles*.

Warhol did not believe in the veneration of art for art's sake, or that fine art should be produced just for rich connoisseurs. He used the silk screen process to ensure that his works could be reproduced again and again and remarked that 'America started the tradition where the richest consumers buy essentially the same things as the poorest.' Though he was referring

to Coca Cola, this belief extended to his art. He used assistants and collaborators to produce his works, manufacturing the silk screens in his infamous 'Factory' in New York. A meeting place for artists and bohemian hangers-on, it was also the scene of extravagant parties.

In 1965, Warhol announced his retirement from art, in order to concentrate on film-making and music. He became the manager of the Velvet Underground rock group and designed their first album cover, *The Velvet Underground and Nico*, in 1967. He directed more than 60 movies, all avant-garde and experimental works, that challenged the viewer. His earliest films, such as *Sleep* (showing a man sleeping for six hours), were silent and almost entirely static, but after Warhol was shot by one of his actors in 1968, he surrendered more control to his assistant, Paul Morrissey. Movies such as *Chelsea Girls*, *Flesh* and *Trash* attracted a wider audience.

Increasingly reclusive, Warhol maintained a remote public face, but remained a cult figure in the New York art scene during the 1970s and 1980s.

Since his death, in 1987, his works have continued to command high prices and in 1994, the Warhol Museum opened in his home town of Pittsburgh.

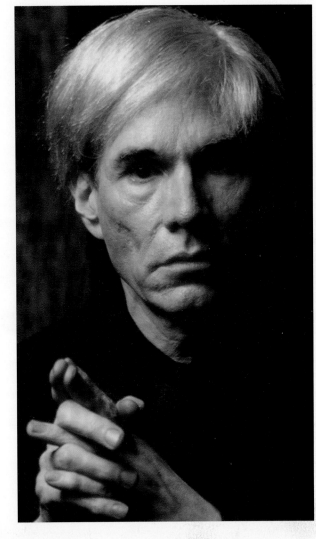

Left and below: Avant-garde and iconoclastic, Warhol and his work were always interesting and provocative.

Shane Warne

The foremost Australian cricketer of his generation, Shane Warne is regarded as one of the finest bowlers in the history of the game. His fearsome legbreak googly bowling has confounded some of the best international cricketers and forced many batsmen to rethink their game.

Warne began his cricket career as a schoolboy, graduating to the University of Melbourne Cricket Club in 1983. His early skill earmarked him for future glory and he was selected to train at the Australian Cricket Academy in Adelaide. His Test match debut, in January 1992, against India, was disappointing. But 18 months later, he established what became his trademark style, when he bowled English veteran Mike Gatting out with the opening ball of a Test match at Old Trafford, Manchester. A piercingly accurate wrist-spinner, Warne's ball became known as the 'Ball of the Century' and was as astonishing, as it was dramatic, seeing off one of England's finest batsmen.

Warne had grown up watching the dominance of international fast bowlers, but he almost singlehandedly revived the leg spin, a tricky maneuver which had almost died out, because it is so difficult to execute successfully. Batsman feared Warne – who was nicknamed the 'Sultan of Spin' – enabling him to establish a psychological dominance that spooked many men, even before he had bowled them his first ball.

Warne's batting was as aggressive as his bowling – he scored over 3,000 Test runs – and he also proved to be a highly successful slip fielder with an uncanny ability to catch balls, but it is his bowling that has toppled records. In 2004, he became only the second cricketer to take 500 Test wickets and just over a year later, became the first player to take 600.

Warne retired from international cricket in 2007, but continued to play for Hampshire in English county cricket and latterly, for the Rajasthan Royals in the Indian Premier League. He is also a respected commentator. His cricketing accolades are impressive, from the Wisden Cricketer of the Year in 1994 to his selection as one of the five Wisden Cricketers of the Century in 2000, alongside Viv Richards, Jack Hobbs, Don Bradman and Gary Sobers.

In a game that distinguishes between gentlemen and players, Warne is definitely among the latter. Ferociously competitive, he is a larger-than-life figure, whose career has seen its fair share of controversy – he was banned for a year in 2003, for failing a drugs test. His flamboyant personality meant that he was never elevated to captain the Australian Test side. This was a shame, because when he captained the Australian side in one-day internationals, he proved to be an inspiring leader, taking the team to ten victories out of 11 matches. Putting his shortcomings aside, many commentators agree that he is one of cricket's great icons.

Right: Warne was the unassailable colossus of Australian cricket in the 1990s and early years of the 21st century.

Overleaf: Warne celebrates his 700th test wicket, 2006.

Born Shane Keith Warne
September 13, 1969
Upper Ferntree Gully,
Victoria, Australia

Stevie Wonder

Born Stevland Hardaway
Judkins
May 13, 1950
Saginaw, Michigan, USA

A star since the age of 13, when he had his first No. 1 hit, Stevie Wonder has proved to be one of the most enduring talents in the music business. The winner of 22 Grammy awards, he has been an innovative, influential and pioneering force in the world of popular music.

Blind from birth, Stevie showed exceptional musical talents from an early age, when he sang in his church choir and played harmonica and piano. He was introduced to the legendary Berry Gordy of Motown Records and was promoted as 'Little Stevie Wonder,' releasing his first single, in 1961, at the age of 11. At 13, he became the youngest person to achieve a No. 1 (a record that still stands) with his third single, *Fingertips (Pt. 2)*, for which he sang and played bongos and harmonica. He went on to have a number of Top Ten hits in the 1960s, including *For Once in My Life* (1968), *My Cherie Amour* (1969) and *Yester-Me, Yester-You, Yesterday* (1969).

Having dropped the 'Little' in the mid-1960s, Stevie Wonder renegotiated his contract with Motown in 1971, capitalizing on his success to demand total artistic control. He had proved with the 1970 album *Signed, Sealed & Delivered* that he could handle every aspect of a recording studio, writing his own material, playing most of the instruments himself and acting as his own producer and arranger. Gradually drawing on more exotic influences, he incorporated African and Latin rhythms with gospel, jazz and R&B influences

on *Music of My Mind* (1972). He began to use synthesizers, which became a signature of his sound. His next album, *Talking Book*, featured two of his best-loved No. 1 singles, *Superstition* and *You Are the Sunshine of My Life*.

Wonder overcame a serious car crash in 1973 to resume concerts and recording and despite his relative youth, was acknowledged as an important influence on musicians, from Jeff Beck to Bob Marley. Many of his songs have been covered by bands, such as The Jacksons and he is respected throughout the industry as a major songwriter, performer and producer.

Wonder recorded more sporadically in the 1980s, but returned time and again to political and social themes, such as his plea for an international holiday in memory of Martin Luther King, *Happy Birthday* (1980). He performed with

countless other international stars – Elton John, Michael Jackson, Gladys Knight and Julio Iglesias among others – and in 1984, won an Oscar for Best Original Song for *I Just Called to Say I Love You* from the movie *The Woman in Red.*

Aside from his outstanding musical achievements, Wonder is well known for his extensive humanitarian works for anti-apartheid, AIDS and children's charities. Held in affectionate respect and admiration by peers, critics and fans alike, Stevie Wonder is one of the pivotal figures in popular music.

Left: 'Little' Stevie Wonder playing the harmonica, early in his career, during the 1960s.

Below: Stevie Wonder performs at the 25th Victoires de la Musique ceremony, held at the Zenith in Paris, 2010.

Tiger Woods

Born Eldrick Tont Woods
December 30, 1975
Cypress, California, USA

Tiger Woods is one of the most successful professional golfers of all time. He has won 14 major golf championships and achieved more major career victories than any other current player.

Woods was a golfing prodigy, who showed tremendous talent when only a toddler and went on to win a number of amateur Junior World Golf Championships, encouraged by his father, Earl. He obtained a golf scholarship to Stanford University in 1994, but left in 1996 when he turned professional. He immediately displayed the qualities that have helped him throughout his career: determination, drive and astonishing talent.

In 1997, Woods shocked the golfing world by winning the Augusta Masters Tournament at the age of 21, the youngest player ever to do so and the first to win it at his first attempt. Since then, he has won three further Masters titles (in 2001, 2002 and 2005); the US Open (2000, 2002 and 2008); the British Open (2000, 2005 and 2006); and the PGA Championship (1999, 2000, 2006 and 2007). He has earned over $111 million in prize money, more than any other player and has more major championships to his name than any golfer, other than the legendary Jack Nicklaus. The only tournament in which he has failed to excel is the Ryder Cup, the biennial team effort of the golfing calendar. The list of his career achievements is long, but suffice to say, he has spent more weeks as the golfing No. 1 than any other player.

Despite his incredible victories, Woods remains, at heart, a cautious player. He was one of the first golfers to dedicate hours to physical training and he plays fewer tournaments than most of his contemporaries, focusing his efforts on preparing really well for the big games.

Until 2009, Woods seemed to be the epitome of the restrained, ice-cool athlete, totally dedicated to his sport, but a series of misjudgments in his personal life gave rise to intense media speculation and showed the world that he was, after all, human. He announced a break from competitive golf in December 2009. In a rare televised speech, he acknowledged that he owed much of his success to his upbringing as a Buddhist, which 'teaches me to stop following every impulse and to learn restraint. Obviously I lost track of what I was taught,' he said, ruefully, in 2010.

Nevertheless, Woods has achieved the impossible – making golf sexy. Aside from his extraordinary talent, he is the most photogenic and charismatic international golfer in a generation and TV viewing figures go up dramatically when he plays. One of the most famous athletes in the world, he has become a multimillionaire, not only through his prize money, but also from corporate endorsement and sponsorship, notably from Nike. His career seems likely to continue for some years to come.

Left: Dedicated and hard-working, Woods spends long hours practicing and training.

Below: Tiger Woods hits the ball down the fairway in 2003, at the Torrey Pines Golf Course. He won the tournament with a score of 272.

Credits

All pictures are courtesy of Corbis Images, with individual photographers and additional agencies credited below.

Front Cover: Main Image, Sunset Boulevard, inset's (top to bottom) Michael Dalder, Peter Tarnoff/Retna Ltd, Pool Photograph, Sunset Boulevard, Michael Ochs Archives, Sunset Boulevard.
Back Cover: CinemaPhoto, Sunset Boulevard, Sunset Boulevard.

1	Brooks Kraft
2	Sunset Boulevard
6-7	Lynn Goldsmith
8, 9, 10	Bettmann
11	Jean-François Rault/Kipa
12	Jean-Marie Leroy/Sygma
13	Victor Lerena/epa
14	(L) Sunset Boulevard; (top) Geoffrey Clements
15	John Springer Collection
16	Andy Rain/epa
17, 18	Hulton-Deutsch Collection
19	Michael Ochs Archives
20	Bettmann
21	Gianni Ciaccia/Sygma
22	Darren Whiteside
23	Victor Fraile
24	Neal Preston
25	Corbis
26, 27	Sunset Boulevard
28, 29	Neal Preston
30	Bettmann
31	Hulton-Deutsch Collection
32	Sunset Boulevard
33	Bettmann
34	Neal Preston
35	Laura Levine
36	Brooks Kraft
37	Soren Stache/epa
38, 39	Bettmann
40, 41	John Springer Collection
42	Bettmann
43	Corbis
44	Steve Pope/epa
45	Roger Ressmeyer
46	Charles Peterson/Retna Ltd
47	Andy King/Sygma
48, 49	Sunset Boulevard
50	Bettmann
51-2	Underwood & Underwood
53	John Bryson/Sygma
54	Lion's Gate Films/Bureau L.A. Collection
55, 56-7	Sunset Boulevard
58-9	Bettmann
60	Peter Andrews
61	Bureau L.A. Collection
62-3	Alessandra Benedetti
64	Douglas Kirkland
65	Photo B.D.V.
66, 67	Bettmann
68	Michael Ochs Archives
69	Hulton-Deutsch Collection
70	Cat's Collection
71, 72-3	Sunset Boulevard
74	Underwood & Underwood
75	Bettmann
76, 77, 78-9	Sunset Boulevard
80	CinemaPhoto
81	Liz Hafalia/San Francisco Chronicle
82	Jim Bourg
83	Tony Korody/Sygma
84	CinemaPhoto
85	Sunset Boulevard
86, 87	Bettmann
88	CinemaPhoto
89	Douglas Kirkland
90	Doug Wilson
91	George Steinmetz
92	Corbis
93	Neal Preston
94	CinemaPhoto
95	Sunset Boulevard
96	Michael Nicholson
97	Swim Ink 2, LLC
98	Grant Smith
99	Rune Hellestad
100	Steffen Kugler/epa
101	Michael S. Yamashita
102	William James Warren/Science Faction
103	Peter Tarnoff/Retna Ltd
104	Douglas Kirkland
105	Derek Hudson/Sygma (L); Sunset Boulevard (R)
106	Bettmann
107	Morton Beebe
108	Michael Dalder
109	Henry Diltz
110-111	Bob King
112	Tomasso DeRosa
113	Frank Trapper
114	Robert Eric/Corbis Sygma
115	Michael Ochs Archives
116	Bettmann
117	Wally McNamee
118	René Maestri/Sygma
119	Bettmann
120	Ted Streshinsky
121, 122, 123	Bettmann
124	Hulton-Deutsch Collection
125	Henry Diltz
126-7	John Springer Collection
128	Hulton-Deutsch Collection
129	Sunset Boulevard
130	Simone Cecchetti
131	Neal Preston
132	Bernard Barbereau/Sygma
133	Robbie Jack
134	Jeff Albertson
135	Michael Ochs Archives
136	CinemaPhoto
137	Sunset Boulevard
138	Alain Keler/Sygma
139	Denis O'Regan
140	Neal Preston
141	Neal Preston
142, 143	Pascal Della Zuana/Sygma
144	Daniel Deme/epa
145	Eric Robert/Corbis Sygma
146, 147	Sunset Boulevard
148, 149	Henry Diltz
150	Bradley Smith
151, 152, 153	Sunset Boulevard
154	Jason Reed
155	Chuck Kennedy/Pool
156-7	Brooks Kraft
158	John Springer Collection
159, 160, 161	Bettmann
162	Henry Horenstein
163	Rob Brown
164	Claro Cortes IV
165	Christian Charisius
166	Bettmann
167	Reuters
168	Bettmann
169	Interpress/Interpress/Kipa
170, 171	Bettmann
172	Louie Psihoyos/Science Faction
173	Roger Ressmeyer
174	Richard Smith
175	Frank Trapper
176, 177	Michael Ochs Archives
178	Bettmann
179	Matt Campbell/epa
180-1	Lefranc David/Corbis KIPA
182	Michael Ochs Archives
183	Rick Nederstigt/epa
184	Jerome Prevost/TempSport
185	Philippe Eranian
186	CinemaPhoto
187	Robert Durrell
188	Benoit Doppagne/epa
189	Richard Melloul/Sygma
190	Jay Dickman
191	Michael Ochs Archives
192-3	Gina James/Graylock/Retna
194-5	Close Murray/Corbis Sygma
196	Bettmann
197	Bernard Barbereau/Sygma
198	Shannon Stapleton
199	Ramin Talaie
200	John Springer Collection
201	Bettmann
202	Cardniale Stephane/Corbis Sygma
203	Cortes /Retna Ltd.
204, 205, 206-7	Sunset Boulevard
208	Robert Maass
209	Kapoor Baldev/Sygma
210	Jean Guichard/Sygma
211	Richard Olivier
212	Neal Preston
213	Brooks Kraft
214	Victor Bockris
215	Karen Hardy/Sygma
216-217	Philip Brown
218-9	Philip Brown
220	Bettmann
221	Stephane Cardinale/People Avenue
222, 223	Tony Roberts/CORBIS

Every effort has been made to trace the ownership of copyrighted material and to secure permission from copyright holders. In the event of any question arising as to the use of any material, we will be pleased to make any necessary corrections in future printings.

Project managed by BlueRed Press Ltd